PASTOR'S GUIDE TO CHURCH LAW

"Practical legal handbook for Ministers, Board Members, Administrators and Leaders."

by

BY REV. JOHN P. JOSEPH, ESQ., CCA EMERITUS

LEADERSHIP
Thoughtful, Relevant Leaders From Around The World
BOOKS

Most Leadership Books products are available at special quantity discounts for bulk purchases for sales promotions, premiums, fund-raising, and educational needs. For details visit our website at www.leadershipbooks.com

The Pastor's Guide to Church law: Practical Legal Handbook for Ministers, Board Members, Administrators and Leaders by REV. JOHN P. JOSEPH, ESQ., CCA EMERITUS
Published by Leadership Books
Las Vegas, NV & New York, NY

Cataloging-in-Publication Data is on file with the Library of Congress.
ISBN
Hardcover: 978-1-971546-02-5
Paperback: 978-1-971546-03-2
E-Book: 978-1-971546-04-9
Workbook: 978-1-971546-05-6

Dedication

To my wife, Jacqueline Coyman Joseph, our children John Mark Joseph, Jennifer Joseph Rivello and granddaughters, Zelda René Joseph and Aurora Jacqueline Joseph.

Acknowledgments

Authoring a book is a major endeavor, so allow me to acknowledge several people who encouraged and helped me, foremost among them being my wife, Jackie. Before we were married, she told me about Jesus, witnessed to me, and encouraged me to attend a home missions work through which I soon accepted Jesus as my Lord and Savior. For more than forty years, she has been my life partner and companion. She has supported me throughout law school, law firms, depositions, hearings, and jury trials. If not for Jackie, I would not have written this book. She is the love of my life and my muse.

I must also acknowledge my mother, Patricia Kurey Joseph; son, John Mark, and daughter, Jennifer, who also believed I could write this book. My daughter-in-law, Salena, and son-in-law, Gerard Rivello, have also encouraged me. Each of them has told me, "you can do it, dad." In fact, Salena sometimes told me "Dad, you need to write a book about these things." Well, Salena, here it is!

My elder brother, Paul Joseph, who is active in the Catholic Church, likewise encouraged me to finish the book.

Their support has been rock solid.

Reverend David Martz, a retired missionary, now deceased, who welcomed to the New Life Assembly of God in Marathon, Florida, and his wife, Shirley, discipled Jackie and me while we were single and young in the Lord.

Reverend Jim Hennesy, who pastors at Trinity Church Cedar Hill in Texas, encouraged me years ago to move out of the pew and become a deacon. He later asked me to join his pastoral staff at Glad Tidings Assembly of God in St. Petersburg, Florida.

Reverend Bruce Klepp, who pastors at Upper Room Assembly of God in Miami, Florida, invited me to be his business administrator help rebuild his facilities after Hurricane Andrew destroyed them. Bruce mentored me in many ways, notably in the power of prayer and faith.

Reverend Dr. Terrell "Terry" Raburn, District Superintendent of the Peninsular Florida District Council of the Assemblies of God, gave me the opportunity to serve as Chief Administrative Officer for the district.

Mr. Herman S. Peery assisted me with liability insurance, and Mr. Gary W. Fagg, CPA, assisted me with this book's IRS and tax sections.

Among others who reviewed and recommended this book are Reverend Wade B. Mumm, PhD (Vice President, Assemblies of God Theological Seminary and senior pastor at Greeneway Church); Mr. Brian P. Battaglia, Esquire, who practices labor and employment law;

Rev. Art Dykstra, Lead Pastor Feather Sound Church.

Mark Jakelsky West Florida Ministry Network AG Executive Secretary/Treasurer

Jonathan Bloom, Esq. In editing

Salena Warnes Joseph in editing

Mari Florence, in editing

They all reviewed and recommended my book.

I also want to also give a shout out to my colleague and friend Richard Hammar, J.D. L.L.M., CPA who would encourage me in my practice as our paths crossed.

I want to thank my editors Faith Burns, Esq. and Amanda Logan who guided my writing, and my publisher Michael Stickler who believed in me.

Finally, and most importantly, I want to thank the Lord who pulled me from the dark into His light.

Table of Contents

Forewords

John Joseph, JD, must have heard the panic in my voice when we first spoke on the phone. That panic was justifiable. I was pastor of a growing church and faced a serious situation—something that could have derailed years of hard work and ministry.

However, within a few minutes, John calmed my nerves by offering a step-by-step solution to my problem. His voice, steady and reassuring, gave me the clarity I so desperately needed. That was nearly twenty years ago, and I've consulted with John on many legal matters since. Each time, he's provided the same level of care, professionalism, and wisdom, helping me navigate situations that might have otherwise been overwhelming.

In *A Pastor's Guide to Church Law*, John does for every pastor what he did for me on that first call; he makes the intimidating and often-confusing world of church law accessible, practical, and understandable. Through his clear explanations and expert advice, he equips pastors to make informed decisions, protect their congregations, and focus on their ministry rather than legal fears.

In today's litigious world, where churches face an increasing number of legal challenges, this book is essential for every pastor. Whether you're facing your first legal dilemma or you've been in ministry for years, John's insights will be an asset to your leadership toolkit.

Wade B. Mumm, PhD
Vice President, Assemblies of God Theological Seminary
Senior Pastor, Greeneway Church
Orlando, Florida

Practical, relevant, timely, and truly appreciated! Thank you, John, for creating such a valuable resource for local church and ministry-related organizations. As an executive leader within a church body, I believe this book is essential for every church leader. The guiding principle I strive to follow and have used to raise my family and lead in ministry is to do right things and do things right. This biblically grounded philosophy is exactly what John communicates: how to honor the law while faithfully serving in ministry. What a blessing!

Mark Jakelsky
West Florida Ministry Network AG
Executive Secretary/Treasurer

I have the pleasure of writing this foreword for John Joseph. For more than fifteen years. John has offered his friendship, guidance, and wise counsel during transformative periods in my career, forming the foundation for my success. As an attorney, I have occasionally observed John's profound impact on his pastoral clients. Their respect for his integrity and counsel was clear to me and confirmed the trust that John has earned through years of dedicated service in both his legal and religious roles.

John's book is a comprehensive guide for church leaders and staff navigating the complex legal landscape that accompanies the creation, growth, and stewardship of a church. John meticulously details a roadmap for understanding various legal requirements, anticipating the challenges facing religious organizations, and seeking professional guidance. This book is where John's work as an attorney and a minister converge to offer wisdom, common sense, and practical guidance.

Whether you're planting a new church, expanding an established congregation, or simply ensuring compliance, John's insights will help shepherd you and your church through the maze of rules and laws that religious organizations must be attuned to daily.

Brian P. Battaglia, Esquire.
Tampa, Florida

(Brian Battaglia has been a member of the Florida Bar since 1986 and represents individuals as well as private and public companies, serving as a leader and officer with various nonprofits, appointee on public boards, and commissioner with a state agency)

As a pastor, my heart is devoted to the church—to shepherding God's people, nurturing their faith, and seeing lives transformed through the Gospel. Yet, as I have learned over the years, the call to pastoral ministry comes with responsibilities that extend well beyond the pulpit. Beyond the spiritual and relational duties, we face the legal and organizational challenges of leading what is, in many ways, a complex entity. It's a unique role where the realms of ministry, leadership, and law intersect.

Despite holding degrees in business and theology and starting in a corporate career, I've often found navigating the legal landscape of church ministry to be intimidating. From governing documents and employment laws to liability issues and financial regulations, the stakes are too high to be careless or uninformed. Stewardship over God's church, including legal and organizational affairs, is an essential part of that responsibility.

That's why I am so grateful for this book. It provides a much-needed framework—a roadmap—for understanding the essential legal concepts and practices every church leader needs to know. Above all, I appreciate this work's simplicity and clarity. This isn't an abstract textbook filled with dense legal jargon or overwhelming theories. It's a practical, straightforward guide designed to empower pastors and church leaders like you and me, filled with tools to navigate these challenges with wisdom and confidence. Every church planter should keep a copy on their shelf, as the book gets better with every read. I was once involved in a church revitalization, and the process of rewriting bylaws, updating articles of incorporation, and changing the church's structure almost overwhelmed me. This book would have helped me a great deal. Fortunately, I engaged the John Joseph's services directly.

In these pages, you'll find principles and actionable insights—a game plan for managing the legal aspects of ministry in a way that honors God, protects His church, and ensures faithful stewardship. Whether your task is addressing the hierarchy of governing documents, maintaining tax-exempt status, protecting the church against lawsuits, or implementing proper employment practices, this book breaks down seemingly overwhelming processes into manageable, understandable steps.

Ministry is an incredible calling and privilege but also a weighty responsibility. As leaders, we are called to be wise as serpents and harmless as doves (Matthew 10:16), and this wisdom includes faithfully stewarding the legal and administrative structure God entrusts to us. I hope this work will be as valuable to you as it has to me—a guide that equips you to navigate the complexities of church law while remaining focused on the mission that truly matters: making disciples and glorifying God.

Blessings,
Art Dykstra, Lead Pastor
Feather Sound Church
Clearwater, Florida

Preface

I wrote this book because I love local churches. Jesus died for them, and we should cherish every church. My law office, the Church Legal Center (www.churchlegalcenter.com), operates in Minneola, Florida, and is dedicated to doing just that—cherishing the churches and religious nonprofits it represents. By reading this book, you demonstrate the same devotion to His church.

This book is based on my experience. I have helped many pastors and church boards navigate legal issues. Some readers may feel I've neglected to address certain topics. This book is not intended to be an exhaustive work but rather representative of my law practice thereby introducing church leaders to certain laws which may apply to their ministry.

In the practice of law, issue recognition is key. **Church leaders must recognize their legal issues before taking steps to resolve them**.

This book presents the church law principles I hope will place your ministry on a more solid foundation.

The following is a breakdown of my qualifications for any curious readers:

REV. JOHN P. JOSEPH, ESQ., CCA EMERITUS

I am an ordained minister with the Assemblies of God, attorney, and Certified Church Business Administrator (CCA) and Fellow in Church Business Administration (Emeritus) now called The *Church Network.*

Cambridge Certificate in Risk Management for Churches and Schools from Cambridge University, England.

I am currently an adjunct professor at Trinity Law School, teaching Religious *Organizations* and *Nonprofit Law.*

In the past I have taught Church Law, Finances and Administration for Peninsular Florida District Council's School of Ministry ordination candidates.

Additionally, I was highly honored to be the inaugural recipient of the Golden Hammer Award, presented by Mr. Richard Hammer, J.D. CPA, "Honoring Those Who Have Exhibited a Mastery of Church Law and Administration." 2001.

As the founder and principal attorney at Church Legal Center in Minneola, Florida, I serve churches, ministries, and charities across the state of Florida.

Education and Experience

I completed my undergraduate studies at Stetson University in 1982 and earned my Juris Doctorate degree from the University of Kentucky, College of Law in 1986. I have been a member of the Florida Bar since 1986 and am admitted to practice in every state court in the State of Florida. I am a member of The Florida Bar Business Law Section and The United States Tax Court.

I have volunteered as a Hearing Master for the City of St. Petersburg and Hearing Officer for Pinellas County, Florida

I have published articles plus a contributing author for Enrichment Magazine, including their special two volume set on Church Management.

I have received the distinctive honor of having been appointed for three terms as a member of the Florida Bar Public Service Pre-Paid Legal Services Committee. I was appointed three times by the President of the Florida Bar to serve as Chairman of the Committee.

For more information, visit www.churchlegalcenter.com

Introduction

For more than thirty years, my love for local churches has driven me to represent many churches. It is God's plan to touch the lives of people. Directed by the Holy Spirit, pastors equip their churches to fulfill the mission of reaching the lost. Church business administrators act as helmsman, assisting pastors with properly steering the ship. Miracles happen when the physical blends with the spiritual. I authored this book to help church leaders identify their legal issues offering them practical advice.

Rather than a comprehensive guide, this book is a glimpse into my law practice. I endeavor to introduce you to the common legal issues I see daily in my church law practice. My list of clients includes small to large churches with multiple campuses and schools. They are also varied in doctrine and belief systems. Chances are your organization would fit in my client list.

Regardless of the sign out front, churches face the same legal and financial issues. This book will start with the beginnings of the church organization through its dissolution. This is what I call the Life Cycle of a Local Church.

The following twelve chapters cover these topics:

Chapter 1: Church Beginnings & Unincorporated Associations

Chapter 2: Formal Legal Incorporation

Chapter 3: Tax Exemption.

Chapter 4: Governance of Your Church Entity

Chapter 5: Governing Documents

Chapter 6: Record Retention & Inspection Rights

Chapter 7: Interviewing, Hiring, Evaluating, and Terminating Personnel

Chapter 8: Legal Risks Facing Churches

Chapter 9: Real Estate: Leasing, Purchasing and Closing

Chapter 10: Church Lending Options

Chapter 11: Churches and Lawsuits

Chapter 12: Dissolving the Church

The reader will find examples to illustrate a point. You will not find in this book many court cases with long opinions nor lengthy statutes. I have purposely avoided this because I wanted this book to flow with a more narrative rhythm. First and foremost, this book is not legal or tax advice and reading it does **not** create any attorney-client relationship. Every church and leader should retain competent nonprofit legal counsel to guide them in any legal matter and a competent CPA for any tax issue or IRS matter. As every church is unique, so are their legal issues. **I cannot overemphasize the importance of securing competent legal counsel for any legal issue your ministry faces and not depending on this book.**

Now let us begin by seeing how a group of believers meeting and "having church" can become organized in a proper fashion allowing them to legally impact their community for decades to come.

CHAPTER

1

Church Beginnings & Unincorporated Associations

When I receive a call from someone at my law office regarding the formation of a church, it often comes from an individual with current or prior experience in ministry. Such individuals have a general understanding about operating a church, but they usually lack the legal expertise required to establish one. Some of them may work at a local church and desire to start their own ministry; others might be laypersons driven by a life-long calling to start a church.

An Example of an Issue:

Several years ago, I received a call from a pastor who wanted to set an appointment to discuss his church's structure and operations. He had been diagnosed with a terminal health condition and wanted to make sure his church would be in good hands and have a solid foundation before his health deteriorated further. After we discussed his church and its structure, I discovered the church had lasted 30 years without incorporation, which surprised us both. The pastor's church was an "unincorporated association." Furthermore, the title to the real estate on which their sanctuary was built was in the names of individuals who had passed away.

After discussing the above points, and those mentioned in Chapter 2 (Process of Incorporation, Tax Exemption), the pastor made the decision to incorporate.

Resolution of the Issue:

To incorporate, we held a congregational meeting, voted to incorporate, and proceeded to file the appropriate paperwork with the state of incorporation. Additionally, we addressed the issues regarding the deed and title insurance, ensuring legal matters were addressed prior to his death. He expressed immense relief, knowing his church was on better legal footing before he went home to the Lord. After his death, his widow told me our initial meeting had meant a lot to him.

Discussing the Issue - Unincorporated Associations

An unincorporated association is a group of individuals coming together for a shared purpose, such as holding church meetings. For example, if a minister is currently conducting gatherings in a residential property or strip mall without having established a proper legal corporate structure, it is highly likely that the church will be classified as an "unincorporated association" according to the state law.

Being classified as an unincorporated association has more disadvantages and legal consequences because the church is not recognized as a separate legal entity from the individuals who comprise it.

Disadvantages - What's the Problem with Unincorporated Associations?

There are several disadvantages to unincorporated associations.

First, members of such associations may be individually and personally liable for the actions and liabilities incurred by other members during the association's business. This can be particularly problematic if the church faces allegations of sexual molestation, negligent hiring practices, personal injuries on the premises, breach of contract, or other similar matters. Since the church lacks a legal corporate identity, it may not have the benefit of a "corporate shield" or "corporate veil" of protection from liabilities. Chapter 2 discusses this subject in greater detail.

Second, if the state you are operating in does not officially recognize the existence of your church, it can have significant consequences. One major implication is the inability to enter contracts or establish legally binding agreements. This limitation can greatly hinder your church's ability to operate as a well-organized entity.

Third, as an unincorporated association, your church may have difficulty when it comes to filing lawsuits to enforce its rights in court. Without a distinct corporate identity, a group of individuals operating as a church may struggle to initiate legal proceedings. In such cases, all members will likely be identified as plaintiffs in the lawsuit. Likewise, if a member is held liable to a third party due to negligence, the plaintiff's attorney may join the other members as defendants in the lawsuit.

Fourth, as an unincorporated association, the church may face challenges signing lease agreements for space or acquiring ownership of real estate. Even if the church manages to obtain title to a real estate or other property, complications may arise during future title transfers. Questions may arise regarding who should sign the deed and whether the title should be held by the pastor, bishop, trustee, or general membership.

Fifth, while corporations can have perpetual existence, the association may only continue for the life of the existing members.

Advantages of Unincorporated Associations

Believe it or not, there are some advantages to having an unincorporated association for a church.

First, it eliminates the expenses associated with the process of incorporating. Second, since you are not incorporated, you may be exempt from paying any annual renewal fees to the state. Third, you may not be required to elect directors or officers, thereby simplifying the decision-making process. Despite these advantages, however, the disadvantages outweigh the benefits.

Practice Pointer

Just because you are a minister and operating a church, this does not necessarily mean the IRS will recognize your church as an exempt entity. You must either apply for exemption by completing the 501(c)(3) application or follow the IRS requirements to operate as a "church." In my experience, the IRS will assume the church leadership is following such requirements.

IRS Implications of Unincorporated Associations

Will the IRS recognize the unincorporated association as an "exempt entity" or a "church"?

Whether your church is incorporated or unincorporated, it must operate under the IRS requirements.

The Church as an Exempt Entity

The IRS does not require a church to formally apply for recognition as an exempt entity. "Exemption" means two things: (1) the church can receive donations without paying federal income taxes; (2) the donor is eligible to receive a deduction for the donation.

A recap of important statements

A church does not have to formally apply to the IRS to be recognized as an exempt entity but you must follow IRS 14 characteristics discussed later. If you apply for the 501(c)(3) you will receive a letter stating you are exempt.

If you are exempt, you can receive donations without paying federal income taxes and the person donating can receive a deduction for the donation.

What Are the IRS Requirements for a 501(c)(3) Entity?

If an entity meets the requirements of 501(c)(3), it will be automatically considered tax-exempt. Churches and religious organizations, like many other charitable organizations, qualify for exemption from federal income tax under IRC Section 501(c)(3) and are generally eligible to receive tax-deductible contributions.

To qualify for tax-exempt status, the organization must meet the following requirements (covered in greater detail throughout this publication):

- The organization must be organized and operated exclusively for religious, educational, scientific, or other charitable purposes.
- Net earnings (profits) may not be used to benefit any private individual or shareholder.
- No substantial part of its activity may attempt to influence legislation.
- The organization may not intervene in political campaigns.
- The organization's purposes and activities may not be illegal or violate fundamental public policy.[1]

1 Source: IRS Tax Guide for Churches & Religious Organizations August 2015 page 2.

Does the IRS Require Doctrine, Religious Practices, or Beliefs to be Considered Automatically Exempt?

No, the IRS does not evaluate the content of whatever doctrine an organization claims are religious, provided (1) the beliefs of the organization are truly and sincerely held by those professing them, and (2) the practices and rites associated with the organization's belief or creed are not illegal or contrary to clearly defined public policy.

Food for Thought:
Does church incorporation create an unnecessary government entanglement and violate scripture?

Before we leave this topic, let me address something I have noticed over the years. Some in the body of Christ believe it is correct to operate as an unincorporated association since the church incorporation creates unnecessary government entanglement and violates scripture. Such individuals choose to operate this way to avoid government interference. They assume the state control their church. I wholeheartedly disagree. Those who follow this philosophy further say the government should have no say in whether a church exists or not. I can understand this belief, but all a state does is record the incorporation of the church. This argument of state control is a nonissue.

If moving from an *un*incorporated association to a corporation makes sense for you, the following chapter discusses the advantages and disadvantages of creating a church corporation.

Action Points for the Next 30 Days:

1. What is the current legal status of your church?
2. Are you incorporated or unincorporated?
3. Does the church have Articles of Incorporation, and have they been filed with the state? If not, you may be unincorporated.
4. Does the church currently own real estate? If it does, how is the property titled? Is it in the name of an officer or trustee who may or may not be living?
5. Always consult with a competent nonprofit church attorney to verify the organization/church's current legal status and request recommendation(s).

CHAPTER

2

Formal Legal Incorporation

Like the pastor who discovered his church was never incorporated, let us assume church incorporation is the way to go. What is the next step? Many church leaders desire to save money by obtaining incorporation themselves. Please do not do this. Most people are not trained in law, and most congregant attorneys are not familiar with the intricacies of nonprofit law. Often the organizational documents are incomplete, and it costs more to fix something than to do it right the first time. For this reason, retain competent nonprofit legal representation to create your church entity. This chapter discusses incorporating a church with its processes and then tax issues of a nonprofit. The first step is to establish the correct structure.

Discussion – Establishing a Solid Legal Structure – Nonprofit Incorporation:

Establishing a solid legal structure is the cornerstone of setting up a church. While there are various options available, the most suitable path for churches is generally nonprofit incorporation. **The Pastor I mentioned earlier chose incorporation. See the example, resolution, and discussion about him.** This step not only provides a separate legal identity but also shields the members from personal liability.

Understanding Other Formal Legal Structures- But First, Board Structure:

Before proceeding, the leadership needs to determine and outline the type of structure that the church corporation will have. When considering the structure of the church board, keep in mind the following questions: (1) What roles are needed on the board? (2) How big should our board be? (3) How does someone join or leave the board? (4) Is it a member or board led church? (5) Is the church led by one individual and not a board or membership? These questions will help you determine which type of legal structure to consider. Examples include the following:

Sole Proprietorship – The simplest way to operate a business is by sole proprietorship. This is when one person forms a business and owns all the assets and liabilities. They operate it in their own personal capacity. All it takes is for a person to say, "I own a home decorating business," and they are up and running. While a person or minister may initially claim, "I pastor a church, and its name is . . . ," operating a church as a sole proprietorship does not fit for a church. One major reason is that all income **may be** taxed to the individual operating the church or the pastor, with no liability protections. Also, donations may not be deductible.

B-Corporation – Some U.S. states have recognized B-Corporations; these are for-profit businesses with a dual focus on mission and profit. The company's shareholders hold it responsible for generating both a financial profit and some kind of public benefit.

Nonprofit LLC – Limited liability corporations that are registered as not-for-profit for tax purposes are known as nonprofit LLCs. Here a company is formed with one or more "members" who operate the business. I have on rare occasions discovered an LLC operating as a nonprofit when the sole member of the LLC is a nonprofit corporation acting as a "disregarded entity." A disregarded entity is a tax term which implies it will be ignored for federal income tax purposes. I highly suggest speaking with a CPA about them.

L3C – Any for-profit LLC that meets the following three criteria is considered an L3C (low-profit limited liability company): (1) It significantly furthers the accomplishment of one or more charitable or educational purposes within the definition of Sec. 70I(2)(b) of the Internal Revenue Code. (2) It would not have been founded but for the company's relationship to those charitable or educational purposes. (3)

The generation of revenue or the appreciation of property is not its primary goal. The attainment of one or more legislative or political goals is not its aim.

Unincorporated Nonprofit Association – When two or more individuals choose to collaborate to achieve a similar goal, they establish an unincorporated association. If that goal is to make money, the unincorporated association they have formed is a partnership or joint venture. Thus, two or more people getting together to work toward a shared purpose, such as church meetings, is the definition of an unincorporated association.

Membership Nonprofit – With this entity, the church members are the final authority in its function and focus, hence the 'membership' part of the nonprofit. The members typically have voting rights and can participate in governance and decision-making processes of the organization. This structure allows for a sense of community and involvement of members. The members have a stake in the organization's activities and directions.

Sole Leader, Director, or Trustee-Led Nonprofit – Here, the governance and decision-making authority primarily rests with either one leader or a board of directors or trustees. The directors or trustees (i.e., elected or appointed) are responsible for overseeing the operations of the nonprofit and ensuring compliance with legal and fiduciary obligations, as well as safeguarding the organization's mission and assets.

Corporation Sole – This is a legal structure in which a single individual, usually a religious leader, such as a bishop or a pastor, is designated as the corporation's sole member and officer. It is generally for hierarchical types of church nonprofits.

An Example of an Issue:

Not long ago, I received a phone call from a minister leading a bible study group from his home. He asked about legal issues associated with this activity. We discussed a few of the legal implications of being an unincorporated association, such as inability to contract and personal liability. He asked me, "What do you suggest I do?"

Resolution of the Issue:

After discussing the legal implications of being an unincorporated association, we focused on the benefits of formal incorporation. He agreed to allow my office file the necessary legal paperwork, such as the Articles of Incorporation. He is now a legally formed church, operating under the suggested guidelines with the State of Incorporation and the Internal Revenue Service (IRS). His concerns and fears have been eliminated.

Formal Incorporation - The Clear Choice

Formal incorporation for churches refers to the legal process of establishing a church as a separate legal entity, meaning the entity is recognized by the government. Incorporation grants the church certain benefits and protections, such as limited liability, tax-exempt status, and the ability to enter contracts and own property in its own name. The state you incorporate in lists the newly formed corporation as an entity doing business in the state as a nonprofit corporation. Being listed as an entity doing business in the state as a nonprofit formalizes the church to act in a corporate structure and not as a group of individual members as in an unincorporated association.

The Process of Church Incorporation

The process of church incorporation involves a series of crucial steps. These steps include selecting a legal structure, determining name availability, drafting articles of incorporation, filing the articles with the government agency, obtaining tax-exempt status, if desired, from the IRS, and complying with ongoing requirements.

1. **Choosing a legal structure**: Churches can opt for different legal structures, such as nonprofit corporations, religious corporations, or religious associations, depending on the laws and regulations of the specific jurisdiction.
2. **Determining name availability**: The name for your church may already be used in your state. Your attorney will research if the name you wish to use for your church is not already taken, thus available to be used.
3. **Drafting articles of incorporation or charter**: This legal document outlines the purpose, structure, and governance of the church. The articles of incorporation usually include information such as the church's name, location, purpose, governance, and any specific provisions required by local law and the IRS code.
4. **Filing with the government**: The articles of incorporation or charter are filed with the State of Incorporation, usually the Secretary of State or a

similar department. This step may require paying filing fees and submitting any additional Forms or documents required by the jurisdiction.

5. **Obtaining tax-exempt status**: After incorporation, the church may want to apply for tax-exempt status with the relevant tax authority, such as the Internal Revenue Service (IRS) in the United States or sales tax exemption with the State of Incorporation if offered. This process involves completing the necessary Forms and demonstrating that the church meets the criteria for tax-exempt status.
6. **Compliance with ongoing requirements**: Once incorporated, the church must comply with ongoing legal obligations, such as filing annual reports, maintaining accurate financial records, and adhering to any regulations specific to religious organizations in their jurisdiction.

By undergoing formal incorporation, churches can establish a clear legal identity, enjoy certain legal protections, and gain credibility when interacting with the government, financial institutions, and the community.

Benefits of Incorporating a Church

Incorporating a church (i.e., nonprofit organization) offers several major benefits, including limited liability protection for members, the ability for perpetual existence, access to diverse funding sources, a clear governance structure, and the legal capacity to acquire and manage property efficiently.

Limited Liability Protection. One of the primary advantages is that the individuals involved, such as the founders and members, generally have no personal liability for the organization's debts and liabilities. This means their personal assets are protected in case of legal claims or financial issues.

Perpetual Existence. Nonprofit corporations have the advantage of perpetual existence, meaning the organization can continue its operations even if its founders or key members leave or die. Whereas sole proprietorships do not. In a sole proprietorship, if the sole proprietor passes away, so does the business entity. In a partnership, if both partners die, so goes the partnership. In a nonprofit corporation, perpetual existence allows for long-term planning and sustainability.

Tax-Exempt Status. Nonprofit organizations, including churches, may be eligible for tax-exempt status, which means they are exempt from paying some federal, state, and municipal taxes. Donors to charitable organizations can also typically claim tax deductions for their contributions, which can encourage them to give.

Access to Grants and Funding. Nonprofits can obtain funding from a variety of sources, including grants from government organizations, foundations, and private donations. Many grant programs and philanthropic organizations target nonprofit organizations particularly for financing, providing chances for financial assistance, programming growth, and community outreach.

Clear Governance Structure. Nonprofit organizations usually have a formal governance structure in place, including a board of directors or trustees to manage the organization's operations. This framework provides transparency and accountability in decision-making processes.

Legal Capacity to Acquire, Hold, and Manage Property. Corporations or LLCs can take and transfer titles to real property. The church benefits from advantages when it comes to establishing lease agreements for space or acquiring ownership of real estate as a nonprofit company. With the legal structure of a nonprofit company, the church has an easier time securing title to property. Future title transfers are likewise expedited, reducing hassles. The signatories for the deed are clear, and the title is held in the name of the nonprofit corporation rather than specific persons, such as the pastor, bishop, trustee, or general membership.

Ability to Sue or Enforce its Rights in Court. Corporations and LLC's benefit from the power to file cases in court to safeguard their rights as a nonprofit corporation. A nonprofit company has its own legal identity. This means that the church can take legal action more efficiently without having to include all members as plaintiffs (as in an unincorporated association). Furthermore, when a member is judged liable for negligence toward a third party, the breach of duty or negligence normally falls on that individual **member and/or church corporation** rather than implicating other church members.

Designation of Registered Agent. The nonprofit corporation is subject to lawsuits. Noted in your state database is a registered agent who is designated to receive service of process of any legal documents and notices related to any complaints or lawsuits. This ensures that the corporation receives proper notice and can respond appropriately. Chapter 10 includes more information for churches being sued.

Potential Disadvantages Incorporating a Church

Although incorporating a nonprofit organization provides several advantages, it is essential to be aware of potential disadvantages as well. These can include the following:

Minor Government Entanglement. Because the state now legally recognizes the church, some individuals fear government entanglement. This, in my opinion, is unfounded. Although it is true that your state statutes regulate aspects of church governance, it rarely (if ever) meddles directly in church matters. State statutes are generally only applicable if the church fails to provide provisions of governance in their articles of incorporation, constitution, and/or bylaws. This will be discussed in more detail when we address the Hierarchy of Documents.

Costs of Incorporation. Some argue that the costs of incorporation are excessive. The expenses involved are filing fees, legal fees, and ongoing compliance costs. The filing fees by the state and the attorney fees are usually reasonable. Rarely do I see high attorney fees for nonprofit incorporation unless you go to a large law firm.

Complex Governance Structure. The structure for a church corporation is more detailed than an unincorporated association. This requires articles of incorporation, or a charter, with which the church constitution and bylaws must comply. This structure can be unclear and unnecessarily complex.

Increased Administrative Burden. Once the corporation is filed, most states require an annual report to be filed, documenting the names and addresses of the entity, officers, and directors. This is generally not required with an unincorporated association.

Loss of Informality. Since a corporation has clear governing documents, there is a loss of informality since these documents must be followed in the operation of the entity.

Increased Public Scrutiny. When society recognizes the existence of a church corporation, it comes with rules to protect both the members and donors. Each state has a "common law" or "case law," which are court cases resolving disputes the court system uses to guide entity behavior. Also, states have statutes or laws passed by legislatures that give guidance on a church's activities should its governing documents be silent on a particular matter.

In My Opinion:

Nonprofit Incorporation, in my opinion, is the chosen entity method for operating a church. It eliminates the personal liability to members and provides what us lawyers call a 'veil of protection' from creditors. In other words, if the creditor is successful in being awarded a money judgment, they must execute that judgment against a corporation, not individuals. Throughout history, corporations have enjoyed this privilege.

Once a type of structure for incorporation is created, what is the next step?

You must draft your charter or articles of incorporation as required by your state.

What are Articles of Incorporation (i.e., Charter of Incorporation)?

I like to call this document the birth certificate of your church. Once filed and accepted by your state, it brings your nonprofit church corporation into legal existence. The content requirements for articles of incorporation vary by state. But generally, the following are common minimum requirements:

1. A corporate name with proper extension (e.g., Inc.) for the corporation that satisfies the state requirements.
2. The street address of the initial principal office.
3. The purpose or purposes for which the corporation is organized.
4. A statement of the way the directors are to be elected or appointed.
5. The street address of the corporation's initial registered office and the name of its initial registered agent at that address together with a written acceptance of appointment as a registered agent.
6. The name and address of each incorporator.

Practice Pointer

Who owns the Church?

Over the years, I have had several families visit my office about their "family church." Usually, the father founded or started it and has family members on staff and payroll. Although it is not illegal to hire family, I do occasionally discover church property is in the name of the family members. This is a delicate matter when speaking with them. I understand the family has made tremendous sacrifices for the church and basically runs it. But I must counsel them that they do not own the church. It is not a family business. A church is not an asset to inherit but a living entity formed under state law for the community. This often causes conflict between the family and church membership after the founder dies.

Drafting Your Charter or Articles of Incorporation

The articles or charter are the foundation document of the church and must be given professional thought and consideration. Keep in mind the exact requirements of your state may vary, and failure to follow those requirements may result in the denial of your paperwork. How can this happen?

First, as an example, your state law may not track federal law. So, fulfilling your state requirements to establish a nonprofit may not include the language the Internal Revenue Service (IRS) requires for a 501(c)(3) corporation. This may include proper provisions such as "dissolution," "purpose" or "legislative." This language is required by the IRS should the incorporated church decide to apply for a 501(C) (3).

Second, your state statute may require a minimum number of directors or certain officers. This is not unusual due to the fact the state assumes you already know the minimum requirements to incorporate a nonprofit entity.

Finally, creating a proper name is critical and most people do not realize they need to do a name search to make sure your chosen name is not already being used by another church. Filing the articles or charter with a similar name may result in a denial of filing by the state. The attorney can do a proper name search to determine availability of your chosen name prior to filing to avoid this problem.

Incorporation is NOT a DYI Project

First, do *not* do this yourself. To incorporate, articles of incorporation must be drafted. Any person desiring to open a church has two choices. First, go to his own state corporation's website to create the entity themselves. Second, hire experienced legal counsel to draft the articles of incorporation. I highly suggest the second choice.

Hire an Attorney?

I have reviewed hundreds of articles of incorporation. Many lacked specific language the courts and IRS require to verify their proper status. Unfortunately, it is common to omit the specific language the courts and the IRS require, resulting in a failure to meet the standards set by the IRS for recognized exemption.

According to the IRS, for example, an organization seeking tax exemption must have one or more exempt purposes stated in its organizing document. Exempt purposes are charitable, educational, religious, scientific, literary, fostering national or international sports competition, preventing cruelty to children or animals, and testing for public safety.[2]

Understanding the intricacies of the requirements set by the courts and the IRS can be challenging for most individuals. It is best to have legal counsel assist in completing the documents.

What's Next? Executing and Filing the Articles of Incorporation

After creating the articles of incorporation, the next step is to execute and file them. Signing the articles is what is meant by executing them. Typically, the incorporator or person filing the articles must sign the document giving assent to the creation of the church entity. Additionally, some states require the signature of the Registered Agent (RA). This person is designated to receive official correspondence on behalf of the corporation. Typically, the RA is required to be an adult available at a street address maintaining regular business hours to be "served papers" if necessary. Service of process and its importance will be discussed in more detail later. Once all the required parties have signed off on the Articles of Incorporation, they can be filed. Usually, the filing venue is the State Secretary of State Division of Corporations. Be mindful, there is usually a filing fee. Once received and accepted by the Clerk

2 Source IRS Publication 4220 Page 3

of the State, the church corporate entity comes into existence the moment the Articles are filed.

Suggested Next Steps: Securing an Employee Identification Number (EIN) and Opening a Church Checking Account. According to the IRS an Employer Identification Number (EIN), also known as a Federal Tax Identification Number, is used to identify a business entity. Generally, businesses, whether for profit or nonprofit, need an EIN. There are several ways to apply but the easiest is to do it online. It is free under the IRS website (irs.gov), and you get the number immediately. Once you have the EIN number, you can bring the EIN number and your Articles of Incorporation to the local bank to open a checking account to deposit the church's donations and pay its bills.

Action Points:

1. Determine the structure of church corporation you wish to form.
2. Prior to incorporating, verify your church's proposed name is available in your state of incorporation.
3. Hire a nonprofit attorney to begin the process of incorporation.
4. Draft and file the charter or articles of incorporation.

CHAPTER

3

Tax Exemption

Nonprofit churches are incorporated under the state of incorporation's nonprofit statutes. To obtain tax-exempt status, nonprofits need to comply with one of the IRS code sections defining nonprofit entities. If you want your church to be a tax-exempt entity, it must operate as a "church" as required under the IRS code, or you must apply and receive your 501(c)(3) "Letter of Determination."

IRS Exemption and State Nonprofit Corporations

Obtaining tax-exempt status is a crucial consideration for nonprofit organizations, particularly churches, as it opens opportunities for benefits and support. While it is essential to meet the state's minimum requirements for incorporation, it might not be sufficient for achieving tax-exempt status. By understanding the intricacies of tax-exempt recognition, nonprofit organizations can pave the way for financial advantages and establish their legitimacy as recognized entities in the eyes of the law.

Understanding Tax-Exempt Status for Churches

Once an organization is incorporated under state law, the next step is to seek formal recognition of tax-exempt status from the IRS. This involves filing Form 1023 titled Application for Recognition of Exemption. This step goes beyond the state requirements for incorporation. The IRS looks primarily at two tests for the entity to receive its exemption: organizational and operational tests. More on them later in this chapter.

In the following sections, we will explore the process of obtaining tax-exempt status in detail, examine the characteristics that define a church for IRS purposes, and discuss the benefits and implications of achieving this coveted status for nonprofit organizations, especially churches. By understanding the nuances of tax-exempt recognition, nonprofit entities can make informed decisions to further their missions and enhance their impact on the communities they serve.

Establishing your Tax-Exempt Status and Formal Recognition

IRS FORM 1023 *Application for Recognition of Exemption*

Churches seeking formal recognition as a tax-exempt nonprofit corporation must file Form 1023 with the IRS. Once the application is completed and accepted by the IRS, the church becomes a 501(c)(3) nonprofit corporation. Form 1023 is rather complex and lengthy and recommended to be completed by a nonprofit CPA.

Practice Pointer

Churches that meet the requirements of IRC Section 501(c)(3) are automatically considered tax exempt and are not required to apply for and obtain recognition of tax-exempt status from the IRS. Although there is no requirement to do so, many churches seek formal recognition of tax-exempt status from the IRS so they may receive a Letter of Determination. This is accomplished by filing Form 1023 with the IRS. Receiving a Letter of Determination is valuable since it assures church leaders, members, and contributors that the church is formally recognized as exempt and qualifies for related tax benefits. Large donors like to have a copy for their CPA since it verifies deductibility for their donation.

Once Form 1023 is complete, the IRS evaluates the application and looks to see if certain requirements are met.

Meeting the Organizational and Operational Tests

The IRS evaluates an organization's compliance with the *Organizational Test* and *Operational Test* to qualify for tax-exempt status. This is done by an IRS examiner reviewing the filed charter or articles of incorporation for the required language.

The *Organizational Test* requires the entity to be organized exclusively for exempt purposes, as specified in IRC Section 501(c)(3). The *Operational* Test examines whether the organization primarily engages in activities that further its exempt purposes.

Organizational Test

Treasury Regulation Section 1.501(c)(3)-1(b)(1)(i) states that, to be exempt, an organization must be organized exclusively for one or more exempt purposes. It is important for the Articles of Incorporation to include *one or more exempt purposes.* In addition, Treasury Regulation Section 1.501(c)(3)-(1)(b)(4) states that the assets of the entity must be dedicated to further its exempt purpose. This dedication continues during the life of the entity through its dissolution. As such the IRS looks for *a dissolution clause* in articles. This paragraph directs that upon dissolving remaining assets will be distributed only for exempt purposes. So, in the life of the organization, its exempt purpose is stated, promoted, and funded even through its dissolution.

Note: The state of incorporation may not require this language, but the IRS requires it in its organizational documents.

Operational Test

Further, Treasury Regulation Section 1.501(c)(3)-1(c)(1) states the entity will be regarded as operated exclusively for one or more exempt purposes only if it engages primarily in activities which accomplish one or more of such exempt purposes specified in IRS Section 501(c) (3). It goes on to state an organization will not be so regarded if more than an insubstantial part of its activities is not in furtherance of an exempt purpose. So, drafting the correct language is important. Here is an example to illustrate the point.

Illustration

In 2021, a Women's' Softball Team applied for a 501(c)(3) status with the IRS, as referenced in Private Letter Ruling PLR 202105009 (2021) (See Appendix 1) The letter stated that the women's softball team did not qualify for exemption from federal income tax under IRS Code Section 501(c)(3) for the following reasons:

1. **Organizational Test:** The team's articles did not clearly state its purposes and how its assets would be distributed upon dissolution. This failure to provide sufficient information led to not passing the organizational test.
2. **Operational Test:** The team's recreational activities for adults served a substantial non-exempt purpose, which caused it to fail the operational test.

In summary, the entity must consider both tests when drafting its articles of incorporation or charter so it will pass muster and be approved by the IRS. Then it would receive a letter from the IRS formally recognizing it as an exempt entity.

Process Applying for a 501(c)(3)

You can apply directly to the IRS and complete the 501(c)(3) application process. Generally, the IRS will not treat a non-church charitable organization as tax-exempt unless it applies for recognition of exemption by filing a current Form 1023. The IRS will recognize a church's exemption from federal income tax if it follows certain characteristics, which the following chapters address. Generally, an organization required to apply for recognition of exemption must file a properly completed and executed Form 1023 with the IRS within twenty-seven months from the end of the month in which it was organized for its exemption to be effective from its date of Formation. An Employer Identification Number (EIN) is your account number with the IRS and is required to file your Form 1023. Subsequent sections within this chapter explore EIN in more detail. The IRS can extend this deadline if the organization meets certain requirements. The process will take a few months, and the application is rather extensive.

Objections to the 501(c)(3).

Occasionally, I find a prospective client who objects to applying for a 501(c)(3). The objection is usually based on one or two beliefs. First, they do not want the

IRS involved in their church for the same reason some people don't want to incorporate. They believe it violates scripture. I can respect that position, but simply not filing Form 1023 does not mean the IRS will not be involved at some point in the church's existence. Second, understanding filing for a 501(c) (3) is not required under law, the client decides against it.

Regarding the first objection, when a church applies for a 501(c)(3), it simply requests the IRS to recognize their entity as an **exempt** nonprofit corporation, and in turn, the church receives a Letter of Determination. Over the years, I have rarely seen the IRS directly regulate the church in any fashion. Though, I have found the IRS getting involved when the church fails to, for example, pay its payroll taxes; otherwise, **the church** will not usually hear from them.

Should the church file for 501(c)(3) exemption?

Filing for exemption costs time and money, but doing so is the best practice. Should the church decide not to apply, the IRS considers a church exempt if it displays the following characteristics:

1. Distinct legal existence.
2. Recognized creed and form of worship.
3. Definite and distinct ecclesiastical government.
4. Formal code of doctrine and discipline.
5. Distinct religious history.
6. Membership not associated with any other church or denomination.
7. Organization of ordained ministers.
8. Ordained ministers selected after completing prescribed courses of study.
9. Literature of its own.
10. Established places of worship.
11. Regular congregations.
12. Regular religious services.
13. Sunday schools for the religious instruction of the young.
14. Schools for the preparation of its ministers.

Publication 1828, Tax Guide for Churches, and Religious Organizations

The IRS generally uses a combination of these characteristics, together with other facts and circumstances, to determine whether an organization is considered a church for federal tax purposes. The IRS does not evaluate the content of whatever doctrine an organization claims is religious; it focuses on whether the beliefs of the organization are truly and sincerely held by those professing them and the practices and rites associated with the organization's belief or creed are not illegal or contrary to clearly defined public policy.

If an organization meets the characteristics, it is considered a church by the IRS. So as stated by the IRS, the term "church" includes synagogues, temples, mosques, and similar types of organizations.

Unlike churches, other religious organizations that do not carry out church functions, such as mission organizations, speakers' organizations, nondenominational ministries, ecumenical organizations, or faith-based social agencies, may or may not qualify for exemption. These organizations must apply for exemption from the IRS. For further details, you can refer to Publication 1828, Tax Guide for Churches, and Religious Organizations, for more details.

What if I don't want to file a 501(c)(3) is there another choice?

The Denomination's "Group Exemption" or Umbrella

Churches that do not wish to file their own 501(c)(3) exemption but do wish for IRS recognition may have another option: falling under their denominations or fellowship's "group exemption" or "umbrella." This recognizes a church as a member of its convention or denominations exemption. This way you can bypass the process of making an application directly to the IRS. Churches as "subordinate organizations" may want to check with their leadership and determine if their headquarters or general council has obtained a group-exemption ruling from the IRS. If the denominational headquarters has such a ruling, the church may inquire about the denomination adding the church under its umbrella. If no group ruling is available to the church, then making an application **itself** for exemption needs to be considered.

Practice Pointer

According to the IRS handbook, if a church has a parent organization with a group ruling, the IRS may already recognize the church as tax exempt. Under the group exemption process, the parent organization holds a group ruling that identifies other affiliated churches or organizations. The parent organization must include the affiliated church. If the church is included in the list provided by the parent organization, it is recognized as tax exempt without it needing to take further action. Group exemptions are really an administrative convenience for both the IRS and large church organizations who have many affiliated organizations. Churches who choose this route do not receive individual exemption or Letter of Determination letters.

IRS Application Particulars:

Letter of Determination of Tax-Exempt Status

Once the application is completed and **approved,** the IRS will send the church a Letter of Determination. The letter states the IRS has determined the church is exempt from federal income taxes and donors can deduct contributions they make under IRS Section 170. Therein lies the magic language.

What Responsibilities Accompany 501(c)(3) Status?

Charitable Contributions—Substantiation Rules. Organizations that are tax exempt under section 501(c)(3) of the IRC must meet certain requirements for documenting charitable contributions.

Substantiation Rules

A donor can't claim a tax deduction for any single contribution of $250 or more unless the donor obtains a contemporaneous, written acknowledgment of the contribution from the recipient church or religious organization. A church or religious organization that doesn't acknowledge a contribution incurs no penalty; without a written acknowledgment, the donor can't claim a tax deduction. Although it's a donor's responsibility to obtain a written acknowledgment, a church or religious organization can assist the donor by providing a timely, written statement containing the name of the church or religious organization, amount of the contribution, amount of any cash contribution, and description (i.e., not value) of non-cash contributions.

In addition, the timely, written statement must contain one of the following: statement that no goods or services were provided by the church or religious organization in return for the contribution, statement that goods or services that a church or religious organization provided in return for the contribution consisted entirely of intangible religious benefits or description and good faith estimate of the value of goods or services other than intangible religious benefits that the church or religious organization provided in return for the contribution.

The church or religious organization may either provide separate acknowledgments for each single contribution of $250 or more or one acknowledgment to substantiate several single contributions of $250 or more. Separate contributions aren't aggregated for purposes of measuring the $250 threshold. Publication 1828 (Rev. 8-2015) Pages 29-30

Practice Pointer

Once you have properly filed your incorporation papers the next step is to open a file to add all additional documents such as state annual reports. The following step is to secure an Employer Identification Number from the IRS.

Secure the Employer Identification Number

An Employer Identification Number (EIN) is your account number with the IRS and is required regardless of whether the organization has employees. Include the organization's EIN in all correspondence to the IRS.

Securing your EIN is an easy process. To secure an EIN, you need to complete IRS Form SS-4. You can obtain this form by calling (866) 816-2065 or submitting an online version of the form via www.irs.gov.

Some states require the EIN to be filed with the state; once you secure the EIN you may need to update your online corporate records to reflect it.

Once this is complete, you can file your Form 1023 and secure your sales tax exemption certificate if the state of incorporation offers one.

Secure Your State Sales Tax Exemption

Upon incorporating, secure your sales tax exemption certificate if available in your state of incorporation. This certificate will allow your nonprofit to be exempt from paying sales tax on eligible items of purchase needed for your nonprofit. However, such exemption from state sales tax is only granted to certain "political subdivisions" and "nonprofit corporations." This is an incredible benefit offered to nonprofits that can result in significant savings. Check with your own state's Department of Revenue about the application.

To benefit from the sales tax exemption, if available in your state, you must apply for the consumer exemption certificate. Once you have the certificate, make and laminate multiple copies to distribute to staff and church workers. This way, when they make the purchases on behalf of the church, the organization won't have to pay sales tax on those items.

Once you are incorporated and have determined your proper IRS standing, the next task as a church leader is to maintain your church entity and follow your governing documents to properly operate. Chapter 3 discusses methods of maintaining your corporate entity and managing your governing documents.

Action Points for the next 30 days:

1. If your church is incorporated but you do not wish to file for a 501c(3), verify you are following the 14 characteristics which have been identified by the IRS as crucial for the church to be recognized by the IRS as an exempt entity
2. If your church is incorporated and you have decided to file for a 501c(3) church, verify your Charter or Articles of Incorporation contains the required operational and organizational test language.
3. Secure the services of a nonprofit CPA and attorney to assist in these matters.

CHAPTER

4

Governance of Your Church Entity

Your governing documents must describe how your church is governed. They guide all levels of ministry operations. Does the membership have the final say? Does the board of directors decide all critical issues? Does one family run everything? Maybe a mixture of all? Chapter 3 discusses various structures of leadership and legal standards imposed on governing members.

An Example of an Issue:

I was retained by a church to help with a situation where one of their board members was causing problems by sharing confidential issues with other church members and office staff. This brought confusion and a lack of confidence in the leadership. When confronted, the board member admitted to doing so. He disagreed with certain actions and felt it was important to share this information with third parties.

Resolution of the Issue:

After reviewing the churches governing documents, I discovered there was no mechanism in place to remove a rogue board member, except for a vote by membership.

The existing board was hesitant to take this route because it would involve discussing the matter publicly. Instead, the board asked for his resignation, and he refused.

After careful consideration, I suggested revising the governing documents to address such issues in the future. Additionally, I proposed passing a board resolution expressing a lack of confidence in the troublesome board member and calling for a congregational vote to remove him from his position as a director. The board agreed to my recommendations and proceeded accordingly, resulting in the successful removal of the problematic board member.

Having governing documents outlining standards of duty may prevent errant activities and, if necessary, assist in eliminating them when they arise.

Discussion of the Issue—Decide How Your Church Will be Governed?

One of the most important decisions is how the church will be governed. There are two basic approaches to governing: membership-based and/or board of director-based governance. Each approach has its strengths and weaknesses.

Practice Pointer

Family members on board of directors. Although nepotism or the hiring family members and friends for positions of power or employment is alive and well in the church world, the IRS does not take kindly to the appearance of a nonprofit operating as a family business for personal benefit. Remember, the IRS grants income tax exemption from donations received by the church and contribution credit to the donor taxpayer because the nonprofit entity benefits the local community. It is not supposed to be a closely held family business.

Membership Based Governance

In this type of governance, important decisions are made through voting by the church membership. For example, members have the authority to nominate and vote for the board of directors, and they have the power to remove officers and directors. Additionally, any significant actions, such as purchasing or selling assets of the nonprofit, require an affirmative vote by the membership.

As part of membership-based governance, your church members may have rights, such as the ability to inspect certain documents like financial reports, meeting minutes, and governing documents. Alternatively, if your church does not have membership-based governance, these documents may be accessible to the public. Chapter 4 addresses this in greater detail.

The strength of this method is the idea that members are actively involved in making critical decisions. However, the weakness is that obtaining a membership vote can pose challenges. These challenges may include but are not limited to proper notice, having a quorum, disagreements, and securing the required votes.

Board of Director-Based Governance

In this model, the nonprofit is run by the directors. It is important to note that no individual director has sole authority over the nonprofit; instead, the authority lies with the board of directors. They have the power to nominate, elect, or appoint other directors and can unilaterally decide to buy and sell the assets of the nonprofit. In this setup, there is no requirement for a membership vote.

The strengths of this model lie in its simplicity. The board of directors can accomplish important actions through a straightforward process: passing a board resolution and taking a vote. There is no need for congregational meetings, debates, or additional voting procedures. However, one of the drawbacks of this model is that the membership does not have a direct say in the decision-making process and their voices may not be fully heard.

Mixed Governance: Some churches have a shared governance between the membership and board of directors. In my experience, this type of governance often works well.

Officers

Who are the officers?

Officers are not always directors. However, they can be and at times are. In most small churches and other nonprofits, it is not unusual to find the pastor as both director and president (i.e., officer) of the church. Although, if allowed in the incorporating state, one may be both officer and director. An officer reports to the board of directors. This may sound confusing to the reader, but rest assured, although their roles are different, it works.

What are the Officers' Duties?

Officers have the responsibility to carry out the directives of the board. They are the hands of the board. This is because board members are not involved in the daily operations of the nonprofit.

Titles and Roles of the Officers

Generally, the most common officers and their tasks include:

President: This person may also have the title of chief executive officer or senior pastor. They will be tasked with performing oversight on the daily operations of the organization. He would oversee staff and make sure the entity performs its function as outlined in its governing documents. The president will usually report directly to the board of directors.

Vice President: This person will stand in for the president when needed. They will usually be tasked with certain projects to assist the president in their role of chief overseer.

Treasurer: This person is responsible for the financial affairs of the nonprofit. This may include collecting tithes and donations/offerings then providing financial reporting to the board of directors and IRS. Keeping accurate financial records is critical to the health of any organization. This office usually requires a person with specialized knowledge in this area. This officer may have a bookkeeper or CPA assist them.

Secretary: This person is tasked with keeping and maintaining accurate records of the nonprofit. This may include minutes of membership meetings, board of directors' meetings, and committee meetings. This will include maintaining and updating all legal and corporate records with the governing authorities. Additionally, certain parties such as vendors, underwriters, and banks may require the signature of the secretary on contracts and closing documents.

Chairperson: While this person may be an officer of the corporation, they are responsible for facilitating board meetings.

Electing Your Board of Directors

It's crucial to clearly define the process for electing, appointing, or affirming directors, either in the charter or articles of incorporation or, in the bylaws. I prefer having the charter or articles of incorporation state the election of the directors will be addressed in the bylaws. This approach is simpler in terms of compliance and makes it easier to revise if needed in the future. It is usually easier to amend a bylaw than the charter or articles of incorporation.

Under a board-run governance, the board nominates and elects new directors, typically through a vote among the existing members. Also, in this model, the existing board may remove a noncompliant director without requiring the membership's involvement.

On the other hand, in the membership model, the church members nominate people from their membership, and the final decision is made during a business meeting where a vote determines the outcome.

Each state has a requirement to maintain a certain number of directors. This minimum must be met to properly carry out church business. I suggest verifying the church complies with your state requirements.

Duties of Nonprofit Directors

Once an individual becomes a board member or director, there are certain duties the laws place on them when acting on behalf of the nonprofit. These duties are placed on the directors to make sure the organization itself is protected. Remember, the board member has no real power within themselves but is a member of a board of individuals who operate together for the management, advancement, and best interests of the nonprofit. These duties stem from centuries of litigation involving corporations and are commonly known as fiduciary duties or issues of trust. Three such duties directors must follow are the duty of loyalty, the duty of care, and the duty of obedience. Let us look at each of them.

Duty of Loyalty

The duty of loyalty requires directors to use their authority only in good faith and best interests of the church. This duty involves holding matters in confidence and acting in the best interest of the organization.

This duty is carried out, for example, by keeping matters discussed in the boardroom confidential. Many reputations have been destroyed by board members' loose lips.

Directors also must set aside their own interests and decide every issue as it relates to the organization. With every matter, the directors must ask themselves, "Is this in the best interests of the church?" This ensures that personal interests do not influence their actions, and that the organization's well-being remains paramount.

One effective approach for a director to prioritize the organization's welfare and act in the best interest of the organization is to make sure any conflicts of interest are openly communicated during board discussions. One way this is accomplished is through a conflict-of-interest policy.

Conflict of Interest Policies

Occasionally, situations arise where the personal interests of directors may conflict with the goals of the nonprofit they serve. For example, a church board member owns a construction company but wishes to bid on the construction project for the new sanctuary the church wants to build. As you can see, this places the director in a conflicting position. On the one hand, they want the contract and the deserved profit, but on the other hand, they hold a role as a decision-maker who is responsible for safeguarding the best interests of the nonprofit. These occurrences are not illegal, nor do they necessarily reflect negatively on the integrity of the board of directors. They are simply due to the fact many volunteer directors are businesspersons.

One way to address these matters is to create and follow a conflict-of-interest policy. A typical conflict of interest policy will address the following:

- What circumstances qualify as a conflict of interest?
- How should the board handle conflicts when they arise?
- What role, if any, can the conflicted board members have?
- The process for resolving such conflicts.

Every church should have a conflict-of-interest policy in place. While some churches include this in their bylaws, many have it as a standing board policy.

Duty of Care

Another duty a director must follow is the duty of care. This duty calls upon directors to act in an informed and reasonable manner when deciding on issues and in the management of the church. This duty can be best explained by referring to the guidelines set forth in the Revised Model Nonprofit Corporation Act of 1986, which states:

"A director shall discharge his/her duties as a director, including duties as a member of a committee:

- In good faith;
- With the care an ordinary prudent person in a like position would exercise under similar circumstances; and
- In a manner the director reasonably believes to be in the best interest of the corporation."

Every Director is bound to follow this duty, but the question is, how is this accomplished? The fulfillment of this duty is known as "discharging the duty," which involves carrying out their responsibilities with diligence, prudence, and careful consideration for the organization's best interests.

Discharging the Duties of Care

The Revised Model Nonprofit Corporation Act of 1986 gives guidance on how the responsibility of directors is discharged.

When carrying out their responsibilities, directors are entitled to rely on information, opinions, reports, or statements, including financial statements and other financial data, if prepared or presented by the following sources:

- One or more officers or employees of the corporation whom the directors reasonably believe to be reliable and competent in the matters presented.
- Legal counsel, public accountants, or other persons as to matters the director reasonably believes are within the person's professional or expert competence.
- A committee of the board of which the directors are not a member, as to matters within the jurisdiction if the director reasonably believes the committee merits confidence.

The duty of care requires the director, among other things, to:

- Be well-informed on church-related matters.
- Defer to other board members with specialized judgment and experience.
- Ensure sufficient understanding of important subjects.
- Exercise independent judgment.

Included in the duty of care and loyalty is the duty of obedience.

Duty of Obedience

Directors are obligated to fulfill a duty that entails making decisions for the church in alignment with its officially declared organization's governing documents and the law of its state. This duty can be included in the duty of care and loyalty. When making decisions, the nonprofit director needs to prioritize and learn the churches governing documents and what they say and then follow them.

Discharging Duty of Obedience

Directors are expected to know the goals laid out in the entity's governing documents (i.e., articles of incorporation/charter, constitution and bylaws). In addition, their decisions must comply with all federal and state laws. Finally, having advice from professionals such as legal counsel and a CPA to assist in following the law and the governing documents is critical.

Updating Your Directors and Officers

Many states require the church to file a report annually on their current corporate status. This "annual report" will give you an opportunity to update your church leaders. For example, this may be the names and addresses of the directors and officers. It can also require providing the name and address of the Registered Agent. More on that office later in the book. Keep in mind corporations are generally governed by their board of directors. Such people meet on a regular basis to govern the church entity. To assist them in this responsibility, they appoint or vote upon officers of the corporation. These officers actively work together to ensure that the directives set by the board of directors are effectively implemented. Identifying who they are is often required.

Practice Pointer

When I am engaged by a church to represent them in a legal matter, I first look up the legal entity on the state database and verify they have listed their officers and directors correctly. This also includes verifying they have listed the required minimum number of directors. Also, many churches incorrectly designate their officers and directors. For example, many churches designate their board members as deacons, elders or trustees. It is common to see churches designate their board members as follows:

"John Smith, Elder"

"John Smith, Pastor"

"John Smith, Deacon"

Listing a spiritual title does not necessarily designate them as a director or officer. Consider listing them, if your state law allows, as follows: first as director, second as officer, third spiritual title.

For example:

"John Smith, Director, Elder"

"John Smith, Director, President, Pastor"

"John Smith, Director, Treasurer, Deacon"

Action Points for the next thirty (30) days:

1. Do your governing documents outline how to remove a disruptive or failed church member?
2. Does your church have officers who are elected or appointed? If so, do they have a clear understanding of their roles?
3. Verify your church corporation is up to date with its annual report with your State.
4. If not, find out what must be done to bring the church corporation current?
5. If it is current, look to see if the church correctly designated the Directors, Officers along with any spiritual title on the state website?

6. Do you have someone appointed or designated to take care of the annual report? If not, appoint someone.

Maintaining your corporation in good standing is not difficult. In many states, church corporations only need to file a simple annual or biannual report with the state. Usually this requires an inexpensive annual renewal fee.

If a church fails to keep its corporation current with the state, the state may penalize the church's corporate status or declare the corporate status as lapsed. Some states may dissolve the corporate entity for failure to complete the Annual Report. In legal terms, this is called "involuntary or administrative dissolution." When this happens to your church, its corporation has been dissolved due to the failure to maintain its status with the state. This, along with its consequences, will be discussed in detail later in the book.

CHAPTER

5

Governing Documents

Governing documents are created to assist the leadership in making sure it complies and follows state laws, as well as the church's own beliefs, norms, and rules. Deviation from them can be problematic and often with consequences. Ensure your documents are current; orderly; and available for review, discussion, and updating. Certain states require these documents to be stored in the church office and accessible to its membership.

Hierarchy of Authority

As we look at documents which govern nonprofits or church entities, we need to know which document takes precedence over the others. So, if there is a conflict, such as election of directors or officers, which document should the leadership or membership follow first? We call this "Hierarchy of Authority."

1. Articles of Incorporation/Charter
2. Constitution
3. Bylaws
4. State Nonprofit Corporation Law

Church Articles of Incorporation or Charter

The key document to church governance is its articles of incorporation/charter. It takes precedence over any other governing document in the church. Any time a church contacts me to address a church issue or conflict, I first ask to see their articles of incorporation or charter.

Unfortunately, only about half the churches I've assisted have this document readily accessible. This happens even though state law may require you to keep a copy in your church office for members to copy and read for themselves. Every nonprofit leader should know this document, its language, and its provisions. Do you know where your church's governing documents are?

Practice Pointer

If you cannot find your church's articles of corporation or charter, contact your state of corporation and request a copy. Remember to also request copies of any amendments and/or restatements to the articles or charter. These amendments may incorporate changes including voting, property sales, affiliation, and dissolution, or even name changes to your nonprofit. Anticipate being charged a nominal fee. It is critical to have a timeline of governance of your church for your attorney. Your nonprofit Articles of Incorporation or Charter along with any amendments and restatement is the key document for any nonprofit leader to effectively follow.

Review your articles of incorporation or charter, and determine if the church is complying with current law and church practice. If not, you may want a nonprofit attorney to update them for you. For example, your articles of incorporation may require your membership to elect directors rather than permitting your current practice. Consider amending or restating your articles and/or bylaws to comply with current practice.

Church Constitution

After the articles of Incorporation, a church constitution is the fundamental, underlying document which establishes the governing of a church entity.

I find most church constitutions focus on the belief system of the church rather than on its operations. Operations are usually relegated to the bylaws. Nevertheless, this document takes precedence over the bylaws, so, if they conflict in any way, you need to amend one or the other to comply with your current practice.

I find more churches today bypassing creating a constitution and putting their efforts into only having one governing document, and that is a set of bylaws. I agree with this approach since it is better to follow one and avoid creating conflicts between them.

Church Bylaws

This is your next document in order of importance. Bylaws are written rules for conduct of a corporation. They should not be confused with the articles of incorporation, which only state the basic outline of the nonprofit. Bylaws generally provide for meetings, elections of a board of directors, and operations of the church.

This document is the road map for operating the nonprofit. Every church is different in its beliefs and structure, but a basic set of bylaws usually covers the following:

- Name of Church
- Affiliation
- Beliefs and Purposes
- Church Ordinances
- Membership Eligibility and Removal
- Membership Meetings
- Order of Business
- Government
- Directors/Elders Elections or Appointment
- Board of Directors Meetings
- Officers' Elections or Appointment
- Removal of Officers and Directors
- Deacons' Elections or appointment
- Departments and Committees
- Finances of the Nonprofit

- General Business Practices
- Minister Ordination, Licensing, and Commissioning
- Whistleblower Policy
- Conflict of Interest Policy
- Purchasing, Selling, and Mortgaging Property
- Miscellaneous Provisions
- Dissolution of Entity (if not in Articles or Charter)
- Parliamentary Order of Meetings
- Requirements for Amending the Bylaws

Practice Pointer

I encourage you to review your bylaws. Ask yourself, does this document follow how we operate today? Does it have language or provisions we no longer use? At times, I often find churches' bylaws need to be updated with current practices. You do not want to be dragged into court and have legal counsel establish your current activities **not only do not follow but violate** your own bylaws.

What happens if a church matter is not addressed in articles, or bylaws? Usually, your state statute **will then control**.

State Statutes on Nonprofit Corporation Law

As a rule, if your governing documents, as discussed above, do not address a certain matter, most likely your state nonprofit statute **will address it and could be binding on the church**. For example, requirements for the election of directors. If your church has not enumerated the process, then the statute may tell you the procedure. Therefore, drafting your governing documents with an eye **to legal and practical** processes is so important. Review your documents and ask yourself, "Do our governing documents address such important matters?" If not, fix it.

Language such as the following is an example:

Emphasis is mine:

A director may be removed from office as outlined in the bylaws.

Action Points for the Next 30 Days:

1. Does your church's governing documents clearly outline who governs the entity?
2. Is it clear how the directors and officers are elected and/or appointed? Are there provisions in place to remove a rogue officer or director with little disruption to the church?
3. Does the board of directors understand their roles and are associated with the duty of care, loyalty, and obedience?
4. Verify your church has a conflict-of-interest policy. If it does not, have one drafted.
5. Retain legal counsel to review your governing documents verifying they do not conflict with the law of the state of incorporation.

CHAPTER

6

Record Retention & Inspection Rights

Now that you have created your nonprofit entity and established the governing documents and structure, it's important to consider the next documents your church should keep on record and for how long. In other words, do you have a record retention policy? If not, how will your staff respond to having such a policy? Also, what records must the church produce if asked by the public or congregational members? Who has the legal right to inspect such documents? Does the church have to produce certain records at all? In this chapter we will address these issues.

Example of an Issue:

I was asked to speak with a pastor regarding an allegation involving one of their youth pastors sexually assaulting a youth eight years previous. The allegation centered on the church's negligent hiring and supervision of its staff pastor.

Resolution of the Issue:

When we reviewed the employee records of the staff from that period, we discovered the individual in question had never been employed by the church but was in fact a volunteer adult leader. We used the original insurance policy to determine coverage and secured local legal counsel.

Discussion of the Issue: Record Retention Policy

It never ceases to amaze me how we love to keep things in closets as a cultural habit. Stuff put away from cantatas years past and the like. I am sure you know what I mean and are probably smiling as you read this. What I am saying is there is room for these documents. Whether you have a physical storage room or not, consider saving the documents electronically in the cloud. If your nonprofit does not have a cloud account, then surely electronically keep them on your server. If you do not have a server then securely store them in a filing cabinet with proper security measures. You do have room for these documents. Hold on to them!

Church leaders should consider establishing a records retention policy because the church leadership may need to go back and review past records. The above example looking into past employee records is a great example. A record retention policy needs to be established because different records have varying retention requirements—some may be disposed of, while others should be retained for several years or even permanently.

Think of this policy as a document management strategy for your nonprofit. It is important because it is unrealistic to expect all records to be preserved indefinitely. In essence, such a policy will provide clear guidance to your staff on exactly what to keep and discard.

The key is to determine ahead of time which records merit preservation and assign responsibility for its execution. Some churches have Church Business Administrators (CBAs) who are trained and well-versed in this area. Those CBAs who desire to further educate themselves can connect with *The Church Network* out of Richardson, TX, at www.thechurchnetwork.com. This organization not only offers classes in church business administration but also provides certification as a Certified Church Business Administrator (CCA). I went through this program (currently CCA Emeritus), and I highly suggest it.

But most churches do not have a church business administrator, so this task often is relegated to the pastor, office assistant, or bookkeeper.

By following the steps below, you can increase the chance of a successful policy rollout while minimizing resistance.

Suggestions on Implementing Records Retention Policy

As you may know, you may anticipate staff resistance anytime you begin a new policy. Allow me to make the following suggestions:

1. **Designate a Leader**: To successfully implement this policy, it's essential to have a designated leader who can drive it forward. This person may be a church business administrator, bookkeeper, or executive assistant.
2. **Clearly Communicate Expectations**: Clearly state your expectations regarding policy compliance and provide the reasons behind it. The information in this chapter can assist you in this regard.
3. **Involve Key Stakeholders**: Incorporate key vendors and outside stakeholders in the implementation process. Make it a team effort to ensure smoother adoption.
4. **Establish Execution Expectations**: Set clear expectations for how the new records retention policy will be implemented. Specify a start date for when it will come into effect.

Although I am not aware of a universal standing record retention policy which covers all nonprofits, allow me to make a few suggestions on record retention.

Records to be Retained.

It is a daunting task to think of all your documents and decide which ones to keep and for how long. While everyone has an opinion on this issue, I find the following process works. It's important to note that not all of these categories may be relevant to your ministry. I suggest you divide the documents into major categories such as corporate records, office and employee records, and tax and IRS records. All three categories are permanent records unless suggested otherwise.

Corporate Records

Article of Incorporation or Charter, Amendments, and any Restatements.

Certificate of Incorporation

Certificate of Good Standing

Correspondence from the State of Incorporation.

Corporate Annual Reports

Certificate of Status

Miscellaneous Filings with the State

Constitution and Amendments

Bylaws and Amendments

Annual Financial Reports

Audited, Compiled, or Reviewed Financial Reports

Balance Sheet

Deeds

Membership Lists

Minutes of Membership Meetings

Three Years of Bulletins

Minutes of Board of Directors/Elders, Deacon, and Trustee Meetings

Committee Meeting and Notes

Property Deeds and Records

All Insurance Policies

- General Liability
- Auto
- Property
- Cyber Risk

County Property Tax Exemption Applications

State Sales Tax Exemption Application and Certificates

Office and Employee Records

Interview Notes with Prospective Employees

Applications for Employment

Screening Forms and results

Waivers on Reference Checks

Reference Checks

Notes on Phone Calls on Reference Checks.

Posted and Finalized Job Descriptions

Memorandum of Understanding (MOU)

Employment Agreements

Non-Compete Agreements

Cafeteria Plans

Housing Allowance Worksheets

Housing Allowance Resolutions

Retirement Gifts by Board Resolution (4 years)

Employers Manual

Work Related Injuries (5 years)

Annual Performance and Evaluation Forms/Notes

Employees Disciplinary Memorandums

Termination Notices

Severance Agreements and Releases

Tax and IRS Records

IRS Form 1023 Application

IRS Letter of Determination or recognition of exemption

FORM W-2 Wage and Tax Statement

FORM W-4 Withholding Allowance Cert

941's Employer Quarterly Tax Return

FORM 990T UBIT

FORM 1099 Misc. Income

FORM 8274 Church Exemption E/ER FICA share

FORM 5578 Annual Cert of Non-Discrimination filed by private schools.

Offering Envelopes (4 Years)

Contribution Statements (4 Years)

All other IRS documents

All correspondence with the IRS

This list is not exhaustive so consult with your attorney and CPA on others which may be retained.

In today's litigious environment, it's crucial for church leaders to understand their roles and responsibilities, especially when it comes to managing church records. Many church leaders mistakenly believe that church records and minutes of meetings are inaccessible to the membership or the public, but this is not true. In many states, the church is obligated to keep certain records in their offices for members of their organization and even the public to review.

Usually, legal professionals do not get involved in these types of matters unless there is an appropriate request which was denied by the church leadership or office staff.

Requirements for and Implications of Maintaining Records in the Church Office.

State law may impose specific obligations on your church to retain records in your office, which may be subject to inspection or copying by certain individuals. It's essential to be aware of your state's legal requirements in this regard. To help you navigate this, I'll break this topic down into three main parts.

1. **Required Documents**. It's important to understand what documents you are obligated to keep in your church office.
2. **Qualifications and Inspection Process**. You need to know who qualifies to inspect these records and the steps involved in the inspection process.
3. **Refusal**. You should be aware of the potential consequences if your church decides to refuse an inspection or copying request.

To illustrate these points, we will examine the laws of three different states. We will work our way from the West Coast to the East Coast—California, Texas, and Florida—to provide you with a basic understanding of how these laws may apply. Once the law is addressed, we will look at some practical applications for church leaders regarding receiving and responding to requests.

But before we look at these laws, take note if your state has similar requirements. State statutory law is specific in this area. Refusal to respond to a legitimate request may subject the church to attorney fees and costs. Securing legal counsel is important.

Now let us first look at California's statutes relating to this topic. (emphasis is mine)

California Code on Record Retention and the Right of Inspection

California Corp Code Section 9510

(a) Each corporation shall keep:

(1) Adequate and correct books and records of accounts.

(2) Minutes of the proceedings of its members, board, and committees of the board.

(3) A record of its members giving their names and addresses and the class of membership held by each.

(b) Those minutes and other books and records shall be kept either in written form or in any other form capable of being converted into clearly legible tangible form or in any combination of the foregoing. When minutes and other books and records are kept in a form capable of being converted into clearly legible paper form, the clearly legible paper form into which those minutes and other books and records are converted shall be admissible in evidence, and accepted for all other purposes, to the same extent as an original paper record of the same information would have been, provided that the paper form accurately portrays the record.

Except as otherwise provided in the articles or bylaws, a member may inspect and copy the record of all the members' names, addresses and voting rights, at reasonable times, upon five business days' prior written demand upon the corporation for a purpose reasonably related to the member's interest as a member.

Comment: As you can see the California Code states the necessity of the church leader to maintain accurate records of a general nature: current accounts, minutes of meetings, and membership records. Not much specificity, but it is clear what needs to be maintained. Now, what about inspection rights?

California Corp Code Section 9511

"Except as otherwise provided in the articles or bylaws, a member may inspect and copy the record of all the members' names, addresses and voting rights, at reasonable times, upon five business days' prior written demand upon the corporation for a purpose reasonably related to the member's interest as a member."

California Corp Code Section 9512

Except as otherwise provided in the articles or bylaws, the accounting books and records and minutes of proceedings of the members and the board and committees of the board shall be open to inspection upon the written demand on the corporation of any member at any reasonable time, for a purpose reasonably related to such person's interests as a member. (emphasis is mine)

Comment: What does all this statutory language mean to a California pastor? If you're pastoring in California and fail to address inspection rights in your bylaws your church members have a right to information one might think they are not entitled too. Notice in the statute a member can request board meeting minutes. (Addressing inspection in the churches bylaws may prevent having to produce such documents). Keep in mind the California Statute does require the requestor to have certain qualifications and requirements to satisfy.

First, notice it must be a member of the church making the request. This may rule out members of the public. In fact, your church may have many long-standing contributors and attenders who have never joined your church. But failure to be a member would certainly restrict their access to this information. As the American Express commercial accurately says, "membership has its privileges."

Second, the member must make a written demand for inspection at a reasonable time. A verbal request is not valid.

Third, for a member's request to be valid in California, he or she must have a "purpose reasonably related" to the request. Just saying "inquiring minds want to know" will not suffice in California. The members' interest must tie into the request. In other words, their purpose in requesting the board minutes must be reasonably related to their activities and interest at the church. In essence, the member must have some role in the church that justifies their request for those records.

Finally, two additional points. First, the written request does not have to be made in the form of a subpoena. It may be a certified letter. Also, if a subpoena to produce such records of information has been served on the church, immediately seek the representation of an attorney to answer the subpoena. Second, the churches' own governing documents may be more broad or restrictive in allowing such information. Note the statutes language which states, "Except as otherwise provided for in the articles or bylaws…." A California church may seek the counsel of a nonprofit attorney to address inspection rights in their governing documents.

California Law on Refusing to Comply

In California, if a proper request is made and the church refuses to comply, the Court may appoint an inspector or accountant to investigate. If so ordered and the church refuses to comply, then the Court may order the church in contempt of court. Let us read the statute on compliance:

California Corp Code Section 9514

(a) Upon refusal of a lawful demand for inspection under this chapter, the superior court of the proper county, or the county where the books or records in question are kept, may enforce the demand or right of inspection with just and proper conditions or may, for good cause shown, appoint one or more competent inspectors or independent accountants to audit the financial statements kept in this state and investigate the property and funds of any corporation and of any subsidiary corporation thereof, domestic or foreign, keeping records in this state and to report thereon in such manner as the court may direct.

(b) All officers and agents of the corporation shall produce to the inspectors or accountants so appointed all books and documents in their custody or power, under penalty of punishment for contempt of court.

(c) All expenses of the investigation or audit shall be defrayed by the applicant unless the court orders them to be paid or shared by the corporation.

Comment: Any refusal ruled unjustified may result in the church paying for the investigation at the discretion of the Court.

In summary, what does all this mean to a California pastor? After securing legal counsel, scrutinize who is making the written request and verify their membership in the church. Determine if they have a connection to the matter or legitimate purpose related to their inquiry. This information will be critical and will assist your attorney in responding to a request for records whether by demand letter or subpoena.

Next, let us see what the state of Texas says.

Texas Business Code Section 22.352 - Financial Records and Annual Reports

(a) A corporation ***shall maintain*** *current and accurate financial records with complete entries as to* ***each*** *financial transaction of the corporation, including income and expenditures, in accordance with generally accepted accounting principles.*

(b) Based on the records maintained under Subsection (a), the board of directors of the corporation shall annually prepare or approve a financial report for the corporation for the preceding year.

The report must conform to accounting standards as adopted by the American Institute of Certified Public Accountants and must include:

(1) a statement of support, revenue, and expenses.

(2) a statement of changes in fund balances.

(3) a statement of functional expenses; and

(4) a balance sheet for each fund.

Section 22.353 - Availability Of Financial Information for Public Inspection

(a) A corporation shall keep each document the corporation is required to make available for public inspection as an entity that is exempt from income taxation under Section 501(a), Internal Revenue Code of 1986, by being listed as an exempt organization under Section 501(c)(3) of that code, at the corporation's registered or principal office in this state for at least three years after the close of the fiscal year.

(b) The corporation shall make the documents described by Subsection (a) available to the public for inspection and copying at the corporation's registered or principal office during regular business hours. The corporation may charge a reasonable fee for preparing a copy of a document.

Comment: What stands out is Texas requires churches to maintain financial records on "every" transaction for at least three (3) years. What about inspection rights?

Texas Law on Record Inspection

Section 22.351 - Member's Right to Inspect Books and Records

*A **member** of a corporation, on **written demand** stating the **purpose** of the demand, is entitled to examine and copy at the member's expense, in person or by agent, accountant, or attorney, at any reasonable time and for a **proper purpose**, the books and records of the corporation **relevant** to that purpose.*

Comment: In Texas there are several requirements in order for a person to request inspection of church records. Here is a list of them:

- He or she must be a **member** of a corporation or church.
- The request cannot be verbal but must be made by **written demand.** (Note: Subpoena not required)
- The written request must **state the purpose of the demand.**
- The reason for the inspection must be **a proper purpose.**
- The records must be **relevant** to that purpose.

This then begs the question, what are the repercussions if the Texas church does not keep such records as required and/or refuses to comply with a proper request?

Texas Law on Refusing to Comply: Criminal Act

The church apparently does not suffer a civil penalty under the statute for failing to keep proper records, failure to prepare the Annual Report or for failing to comply with a proper request. But it commits a crime.

Section 22.354 Failure to Maintain Financial Record or Prepare Annual Report: Offense.

*(a) A corporation commits an **offense** if the corporation fails to maintain a financial record, prepare an annual report, or make the record or report available to the public in the manner required by Section 22.353.*

*(b) An offense under this section is a Class B **misdemeanor.***

This raises the stakes for failure to comply with the Texas Statute.

Next, let's see how the state of Florida deals with this issue.

Florida clearly specifies which records the church must maintain and which it must submit. For example, a Florida church must maintain the following at its office:

Florida Statute on Record Retention

(emphasis is mine)

FSA 617.1601 Corporate Records:

(1) "A corporation ***shall keep as record:*** *minutes of all meetings of its members and board of directors, a record of actions taken...."*

(2) "A corporation shall maintain accurate accounting records... and

(3) record of its members

(FSA 617.1601 (5) *"A corporation* ***shall keep a copy*** *of the following records":*

> *"Its Articles of Incorporation or Restated Articles"*

> *Its Bylaws or Restated Bylaws."*

> *"The Minutes of all members meetings and records of all actions taken."*

> *Written communications to all members... within the past 3 years...."*

> *"Financial Statements furnished for the past three years."*

> *"List of the names and addresses of its current directors and officers."*

> *"Its most recent annual report to the Department of State.*

Comment: Florida has a rather comprehensive list of documents a church must keep as a record. Notice the church must keep a copy of all written communications to all members within the past three years. I have observed most churches communicate to their members through a written or web based weekly bulletin. In my experience, most Florida churches have not kept a copy of their weekly bulletins for the past three years in the office.

Now let's look at who can request church records in Florida. Again, like California and Texas eligibility lies with the church member.

Florida Law on Record Inspection

Statute 617.1602

A ***member*** *of a corporation is entitled to* ***inspect*** *and copy, during regular business hours at the corporation's principal office or at a reasonable location specified by* *the corporation, any of the records of the corporation described in s. 617.1601(5), if the member gives the corporation **written notice** of his or her demand at least 10 business days before the date on which he or she wishes to inspect and copy.*

Now what they have access to is also listed and gives guidance to the church to prepare for such a request. Statute 617.1602 incorporates the documents listed in 617.1601(5) as automatically available to the membership upon request.

However, other documents may also be available should the member qualify to access them.

Statute 617.1602 (2) states:

*(a) A **member** of a corporation is entitled to inspect and copy, during regular business hours at a reasonable location specified by the corporation, any of the following records of the corporation if the member **meets the requirements** of subsection (3) and gives the corporation **written notice** of his or her demand at least 10 business days before the date on which he or she wishes to inspect and copy:*

Excerpts from minutes of any meeting of the board of directors,

Records of any action of a committee of the board of directors while acting in place of the board of directors on behalf of the corporation,

Minutes of any meeting of the members, and

Records of action taken by the members or board of directors without a meeting, to the extent not subject to inspection under subsection (1).

(b) Accounting records of the corporation.

(c) The record of members.

(d) Any other books and records.

Florida Requirements of Person Requesting Inspection

(3) A member may inspect and copy the records described in subsection (2) (above) only if:

*(a) The **member's demand** is made in **good faith and for a proper purpose.***

*(b) The **member describes** with **reasonable particularity** his or her purpose and the records he or she desires to inspect.*

*(c) The records are directly connected with the **member's purpose (or** as later under (7) defined as "reasonably related to such person's interest as a member.",*

Comment: Note members of Florida churches can have access to records such as excerpts of minutes from board meetings if they qualify. Take Away: Florida leaders need to determine the *member's eligibility* before deciding to allow or decline access to church records. Should the church decline a member's legitimate request the result may be a lawsuit and possible payment of the member's attorney fees and costs as stated below.

Florida Law on Refusing to Comply

617.1604 Court-ordered inspection.

(1) *If a corporation does not, within a reasonable time, allow a member to inspect and copy any record, and the member complies with any prerequisites to inspection and copying imposed by this section, the member may apply to the circuit court in the county where the corporation's principal office... The court shall dispose of an application under this subsection on an expedited summary basis.*

(2) *If the court orders inspection or copying of the records demanded, it shall also order the corporation and the custodian of the particular records demanded* ***to pay the member's costs, including reasonable attorney's fees****, reasonably incurred to obtain the order and enforce its rights under this section unless the corporation, or the officer, director, or agent, as the case may be, provides that it or he or she* ***refused inspection in good faith*** *because it or he or she had a* ***reasonable basis for doubt*** *about the right of the member to inspect or copy the records demanded.*

In summary the three states we looked at, like others, have requirements for nonprofits to maintain certain records in the church office and requirements for those wanting access to them. Some states offer **civil or criminal** penalties for failure to keep the required records or for failing to produce them in response to a proper request. You may be asking yourself, why the requirements? Social purpose holds nonprofits open to certain disclosure requirements since they are given tremendous tax favored treatment by society, and the members who support them should have rights to certain records.

Practice Pointer

One day, while I was at my law office, I received a call from another attorney asking me if I represented a particular church in his community. I confirmed that I did represent the church. The attorney proceeded to inform me that his client, who happened to be a long-standing member of my client's church for over thirty years and a regular tithe payer, was seeking a copy of the board minutes from the day the senior pastor dismissed the youth pastor. He then conveyed that if I didn't provide these documents, his client intended to take legal action against my client.

After discussing the matter with my client, the pastor confirmed, even to his surprise, that although this individual had been a long-standing tither, she never actually joined the church. As such, I conveyed to the attorney that I couldn't provide him with the requested documents because his client didn't meet the minimum statutory requirements necessary to be entitled to such records or a summary of the meeting. Consequently, no records were ever turned over, and I have not received any further communication from the attorney.

Food for Thought: A Word About Churches Without Membership.

I understand the trend today for some pastors is to have a church without any formal membership. A word of caution is warranted here: Who then is entitled to these documents in this scenario? Is it limited to regular attenders? Tithe paying people? The general public? As the American Express commercial states, "membership has its privileges." How the Court will address this is yet to be determined, but it will within time. If I were to speculate, I would say if a church had no stated membership, then regular attenders and donors may have inspection rights.

It is important for church leaders to know and understand their state laws on this topic and if necessary secure the services of a nonprofit attorney to help them interpret and follow them. This way, if confronted with a record request, the minister will be able to address it confidentially and in the best interest of their ministry.

Action Points for the Next 30 Days:

1. Recognize the importance of records retention.
2. Establish a records retention policy focusing on permanent records.
3. Determine what records must be kept and available for review in your church office.
4. Store your records on the cloud.
5. If you receive an inspection request, recognize who can make it, your timelines to respond, and secure legal counsel before responding.

Record Retention and Inspection Compliance Checklist

IMPORTANT: Faith added this checklist to my book. It looks great and I like it. Please verify with her there are no copyright issues using it. Thanks!

Week 1: Establish Record Retention Policy

[ ] **Goal 1: Develop a Record Retention Policy.**

[ ] Research state-specific legal requirements.

[ ] Define which records are essential for your organization.

[ ] Determine retention periods for each record category.

[ ] Assign responsibility for policy implementation.

[ ] **Goal 2: Appoint a Records Administrator.**

[ ] Identify a qualified individual to oversee record management.

[ ] Communicate their role and responsibilities.

Week 2: Communicate Policy Expectations

[ ] **Goal 3: Clearly communicate policy expectations.**

[ ] Schedule meetings or training sessions with staff and stakeholders.

[ ] Explain the importance of the record retention policy.

[ ] Distribute copies of the policy for review.

Week 3: Identify Relevant Records and Compliance Procedures

[ ] **Goal 4: Identify relevant records.**

[ ] Categorize records into corporate, office and employee, and tax and IRS records.

[ ] Create a list of specific records within each category.

[ ] **Goal 5: Research state laws.**

[ ] Research and understand your state's laws governing record retention and inspection rights.

[ ] Identify any specific legal requirements for your region.

[ ] **Goal 6: Document compliance procedures.**

[ ] Develop procedures for record retention, access, and disposal.

[ ] Outline timelines and formats for record retention.

[ ] Establish backup and storage strategies.

Week 4: Prepare for Inspection Requests and Stay Informed

[ ] **Goal 7: Prepare for inspection requests.**

[ ] Develop a plan for handling record inspection requests.

[ ] Determine how to verify the qualifications of requesters.

[ ] Establish a process for responding to requests in compliance with the law.

[ ] **Goal 8: Stay updated on legal developments.**

[ ] Subscribe to relevant legal newsletters or resources.

[ ] Appoint someone to monitor changes in state laws related to record retention and inspection rights.

[ ] **Goal 9: Review Membership Status.**

[ ] Evaluate your organization's membership status and understand how it may impact record access.

[ ] **Goal 10: Seek Legal Counsel.**

[ ] Identify a nonprofit attorney who can provide guidance and support in the event of legal challenges or complex requests.

[ ] **Goal 11: Begin Record Clean-Up.**

[ ] Start organizing and cleaning up existing records to align with the Record Retention Policy.

[ ] **Goal 12: Educate Staff and Stakeholders.**

[ ] Schedule training sessions or information sharing to educate staff and stakeholders about the importance of record retention and inspection compliance.

CHAPTER

7

Interviewing, Hiring, Evaluating, and Terminating Personnel

Hiring, maintaining, and even firing employees is an important area of church management. Improper hiring and termination of employees opens liabilities. As a result, churches occasionally face lawsuits from prospective or terminated employees. Yes, we will address the often discussed "ministerial exception" and how it applies to your hiring and firing practices. In this chapter, we will discuss the important topics of insurance, interviewing, hiring, payroll, benefits, and managing and terminating employees.

An Example of an Issue:

When you hire an employee, it is important to document the wages and benefits agreed upon between the parties. For example, a couple years ago, I received a phone call from a pastor who was angry and hurt. He explained to me he recently hired his new administrative assistant and was initially happy with the hire. Then, after a couple weeks of work, she complained that her first paycheck was incorrect. She was under the impression her starting wage was higher and told the administrative pastor in no uncertain terms it needed to be fixed. I questioned him about the starting pay he promised her, and he said it was a different number than she remembered.

This caused much angst. I asked him if he documented in writing to her the terms of the hire. He said he did not and had never had this happen before.

Resolution of Issue:

Although it was too late to prevent this event, I suggested to the pastor the next time he hires a new staff member to do the following: draft and execute a Memorandum of Understanding (MOU) outlining the starting pay and benefits along with attaching the job description. Then, place it in the new employee file. This would have either prevented the problem or immediately solved it.

Practice Pointer

The MOU should clearly state it is not an employment agreement or contract but simply a document outlining the mutually agreed terms for employment. It should clearly indicate, if allowed by your state, the new hire is an "employment at-will" and that the offer is not for a fixed term of employment and the employee can be terminated with or without cause at any time. Clearly delineate these important facts with the signature of both parties. More on MOU's later in this chapter. It is critical the church secures the services of legal counsel to make sure the MOU complies with state and federal laws.

Discussion of the Issue: Hiring Employees

Probably one of the most daunting tasks of a new pastor is the hiring of their first staff member. In fact, maintaining a church staff is a constant task for all pastors whether you're experienced in hiring staff or not. Where do you find the employee? Do you go to an employment agency? Hire by advertising?

Hiring In-House for Church Employees

Many churches hire non-ministerial or administrative staff from within their church. There is nothing illegal or improper in this method. The strengths are glaring. First, the candidate already knows your church. Second, he or she has most likely already embraced your vision. Finally, the church staff may already know their spirituality, personality, and qualifications. Alternatively, the negatives of advertising are clear. You may have a candidate who does not embrace your faith nor your vision but has good professional qualifications. Abilities aside, the former intangible qualification in my opinion trumps the latter.

If your church is small and the pool of qualified candidates is very thin, then I suggest you contact other local ministers and churches in your area for people who may be seeking a position. Although they are not attending your church, you run a better chance of them having similar spiritual and ethical makeup.

Hiring Church Members and Family Members of Staff

Nepotism is alive and well in the church world. Many ministers hire their spouses, children, and in-laws for paid positions in the church. This is a delicate topic, but I generally do not shy away from sensitive matters. Nepotism is defined in Black's Law Dictionary 8th Edition as "Bestowal of official favors on one's relatives, especially, in hiring."[3]

Keep in mind the IRS does not look favorably on a nonprofit that is acting like a family business. Are most of your board members or staff members of your family? What percentage of the payroll goes to the senior pastor's family? Better yet, what percentage of the church's income benefits the pastor's family?

Let us remember, a nonprofit is given exemption from paying federal income taxes for the donations it receives because society expects the church to benefit the community it serves. Additionally, the IRS gives a deduction to the contributors.

Do not misunderstand me. There is nothing wrong, illegal, or unethical in paying a family member a commensurate wage for qualified work performed for the nonprofit. But over the years, I have seen some churches operate as a family business with most of the church's income going to the pastor and his/her family. Be careful if that is you.

Interviewing Prospective Employees

This first step in hiring staff can seem daunting to the inexperienced, so allow me to say a few words about this process. On the legal front, be careful with the questions of an interviewee.

According to the Equal Employment Opportunity Commission (EEOC):

(emphasis is mine)

3 Henry Black, Black's Law Dictionary: 8th Edition. St. Paul, MN, West, a Thomson business, 2004, page 1066.

"Before a job offer has been made, you can't ask questions about an applicant's disability or questions that are likely to reveal whether an applicant has a disability. This is true even if the disability is obvious. You can ask the applicant to describe or demonstrate how they would perform specific job tasks.

For example, you can't ask an applicant:

- *Do you have a disability?*
- *What medications are you currently taking?*
- *Have you filed any workers' compensation claims?*

However, you can ask an applicant if he will need a reasonable accommodation during the application process or on the job, in certain circumstances:

- *You can ask an applicant with a disability which is obvious or which the applicant disclosed if he will need assistance with or a change to the application process* because of his disability; and
- *You can ask an applicant with a disability which is obvious or which the applicant disclosed if they will need a change to the work environment or to the way a job is usually done, if you reasonably believe that he will need a reasonable accommodation to perform the job.*

You also can't ask questions about an applicant's genetic Information*, such as the applicant's family medical history or receipt of genetic tests or genetic counseling.*

For example, you can't ask an applicant:

- *Have any of your close relatives had a heart attack or been diagnosed with a heart condition?*
- *Do mental health conditions such as bipolar disorder, depression, or schizophrenia run in your family?*
- *Have you had genetic tests to determine whether you are at risk of cancer?*

These rules apply to any communications with or about the applicant, including application Forms, interviews, and reference checks.

These rules also apply whether you are seeking information from the applicant or from someone else, such as the applicant's doctor, former employers, friends, or family."[4]

4 EEOC. "What can't I ask when hiring?". U.S. Equal Employment Opportunities Commission. n.d. https://www.eeoc.gov/employers/small-business/4-what-cant-i-ask-when-hiring

Not Offering the Job.

A few comments about passing on the job prospect. First, realize you must keep your notes from the interview. Always open a file on any new hires or those you pass over. The legal reason is clear. The interviewee may believe you did not offer them the job because you discriminated against them. Common allegations are racial, age, and gender discrimination. Yet the interviewer may have determined he or she lacked experience, was not qualified, or would not make a good fit on the team. This should be in your notes.

It is important to keep notes from your interview with any interviewee so you can refer to them if a complaint is filed against the church. This is done by filing a complaint with the EEOC or state or local agency who is tasked with this process. There are time limits to file. The process requires the complainant to make a signed statement asserting the church was engaged in employment discrimination and requests the EEOC to take remedial action. This complaint must be done, except for the Equal Pay Act before a lawsuit can be filed against the church for unlawful discrimination. The time frames are also listed below for your reference.

Churches must be aware of certain federal laws protecting employees. Keep in mind, many states have corresponding statutes the church must also follow:

Title VII of the Civil Rights Act of 1964 which prohibits discrimination in employment for race, color, sex, religion, and national origin, if the employer is engaged in commerce having at least 15 employees. Currently the EEOC is expanding their definition of "sex" to include gender identity, harassment, and orientation.

It is important to note for churches the Ministerial exception still applies.

Federal Americans with Disability Act (ADA) prohibits employers who are engaged in interstate commerce, with at least 15 employees, to discriminate against disabled persons. Churches are allowed to give preference to non-disabled members based on their faith. But keep in mind some states have their own legislation and exemptions which must be followed. Consult with an Employment Law attorney to check your state law regarding application of the Federal and/or State ADA type provisions.

Federal Age Discrimination in Employment Act, which prohibits employers with 20 or more employees who are engaged in interstate commerce to discriminate based on age of an employee or applicant 40 years old or older.

The EEOC gives clear direction to employees who feel they have been discriminated against and makes the following statement:

"If you believe you have been discriminated against by an employer, labor union or employment agency when applying for a job or while on the job because of your race, color, sex, religion, national origin, age, or disability, or believe that you have been discriminated against because of opposing a prohibited practice or participating in an equal employment opportunity matter, you may file a charge of discrimination with the U.S. Equal Employment Opportunity Commission (EEOC).

Charges may be filed in person, by mail or by telephone by contacting the nearest EEOC office. *If there is not an EEOC office in the immediate area, call toll free 800-669-4000 or 800-669-6820 (TDD) for more information. To avoid delay, call or write beforehand if you need special assistance, such as an interpreter, to file a charge.*

There are strict time frames in which charges of employment discrimination must be filed. To preserve the ability of EEOC to act on your behalf and to protect your right to file a private lawsuit, should you ultimately need to adhere to the following guidelines when filing a charge."

Title VII of the Civil Rights Act of 1964 (Title VII) charges must be filed with EEOC within 180 days of the alleged discriminatory act. However, in states or localities with anti-discrimination laws and agencies authorized to grant or seek relief, a charge must be presented to that state or local agency. Furthermore, in such jurisdictions, you may file charges with EEOC within 300 days of the discriminatory act, or 30 days after receiving notice that the state or local agency has terminated its processing of the charge, whichever is earlier. When charges or complaints are filed beyond these time frames, the complainant may not be able to obtain any remedy. However, note that each agency has its own unique time frames.

Federal Age Discrimination in Employment Act (ADEA) – The time requirements for filing a charge are the same as those for Title VII and the ADA.

Equal Pay Act (EPA) – Individuals are not required to file an EPA charge with EEOC before filing a private lawsuit. However, charges may be filed with EEOC, and some cases of wage discrimination also may be violations of Title VII. If an EPA charge is filed with EEOC, the procedure for filing is the same as for charges brought under Title VII. However, the time limits for filing in court are different under the EPA. "[5]

5 EEOC. "Filing a charge". U.S. Equal Employment Opportunities Commission. n.d. https://www.eeoc.gov/fact-sheet/filing-charge

What types of discrimination does the EEOC deal with? According to the EEOC the following are the various types they investigate:

- Age
- Disability
- Equal Pay/Compensation
- Genetic Information
- Harassment
- National Origin
- Pregnancy
- Race/Color
- Religion
- Retaliation
- Sex
- Sexual Harassment
- Sexual Orientation and Identity[6]

State laws also apply. States and legal agencies must also comply with civil rights and discrimination laws.

As stated on the EEOC website under the heading:

Pre-Employment Inquiries and Religious Affiliation or Beliefs

"Questions about an applicant's religious affiliation or beliefs (unless the religion is a bona fide occupational qualification (BFOQ)), are generally viewed as non-job-related and problematic under federal law. Religious corporations, associations, educational institutions, or societies are exempt from the federal laws that EEOC enforces when it comes to the employment of individuals based on their particular religion. In other words, an employer whose purpose and character is primarily religious is permitted to lean towards hiring persons of the same religion. This exception relieves religious organizations only from the ban on employment discrimination based on religion. It does not exempt such organizations from employing individuals due to their race, gender, national

6 EEOC. "Discrimination by Type". U.S. Equal Employment Opportunities Commission. n.d. https://www.eeoc.gov/discrimination-type

origin, disability, color, and/or age. Other employers should avoid questions about an applicant's religious affiliation, such as place of worship, days of worship, and religious holidays and should not ask for references from religious leaders, e.g., minister, rabbi, priest, imam, or pastor."[7]

Since the law is applied on a case-by-case basis, I strongly urge securing the services of an experienced employment and labor law attorney to guide your organization in these matters. This is especially true if you have been served a complaint.

The EEOC also deals with matters of discrimination against people with disabilities. According to the EEOC:

Emphasis is mine.

"In general, you may not consider an ***applicant's disability*** when making hiring decisions. There are limited exceptions to this rule. In limited circumstances, you may consider an applicant's disability when making hiring decisions.

You may decline to hire an applicant with a disability if he is unable to perform the ***essential functions*** of the job, with or without a *reasonable accommodation.*

You may reject an applicant with a disability if he would impose a significant risk of substantial harm to health or safety, and the risk of harm can't be limited or eliminated with a reasonable accommodation."[8] *But remember some states have their own disability protections and exemptions to follow.*

Practice Pointer

What happens when an aggrieved person files charges with the Equal Employment Opportunity Commission or EEOC? The EEOC will then review the facts and determine if there was discrimination. If in their judgement there discrimination then the Commission will issue a right-to-sue letter, alleging the violation of the person's civil rights. Then a lawsuit can be filed in a federal district court under the relevant Civil Rights Act.

As such, I suggest retaining interview notes and employment applications. Should your church find itself with an EEOC "Right to Sue Letter," immediately

7 EEOC. "Pre-Employment Inquiries and Religious Affiliation or Beliefs". U.S. Equal Employment Opportunities Commission. n.d. https://www.eeoc.gov/pre-employment-inquiries-and-religious-affiliation-or-beliefs

8 EEOC. "Hiring Decisions Based on Disability", U.S. Equal Employment Opportunity Commission. n.d. https://www.eeoc.gov/employers/small-business/hiring-decisions-based-disability

notify your Liability Insurance carrier for possible coverage and consult with an employment and labor law attorney for guidance.

Practice Pointer

Most churches' liability policies I have seen have excluded employment practices coverage. Often, I see it as a Rider to be attached for an additional premium. So do not assume the church has liability coverage for an employment claim or lawsuit.

Hiring the Employee and Opening Employee File

Let us say you have chosen the best qualified candidate for the position. What is next? The first thing is to inform them of the offer and ask them, if they are currently employed, how they wish to exit their current position. Not much is said about this but as the old saying goes, "what goes around, comes around." You need to make sure the candidate leaves his/her current job under standard practices, which is usually two weeks' notice.

Do you think the person you are hiring will stay with you forever? They will remember how you wanted their past employer to be treated. In that way, you will be treated.

Once you have decided on the candidate, consider drafting and executing a Memorandum of Understanding (MOU). I mentioned it earlier in the chapter.

Sample MOU

NOTE: It should clearly state it is not an employee contract but just a memo outlining the terms agreed to between the successful candidate and the employer (church).

Names of parties.

Position offered:

Duties of position.

Hours to be worked and where:

Their supervisor______

Start pay.

Effective date of pay.

Benefits offered:

Start day of benefits:

Disclaimer statement this is not an employment contract.

Other issues specific to your church.

Signatures by both parties and dated.

Signing this document protects both parties from occasional misunderstandings. After signature, place the original MOU in the employee's file and provide the new employee with a copy. If you are a larger nonprofit, send it to your administrative, bookkeeping, or human resources department to file.

Once hired, a person should learn how the church office operates, including its policies regarding common concerns such as paid time off. An employee handbook can facilitate this.

Employee Handbook

Employee manuals (i.e., policy and procedure manuals) are important. Although employees may find them daunting, they are essential for understanding a workplace's policies and procedures.

Your employee handbook should reflect the most important factors driving your church's operations.

The following are common topics usually contained within an employee handbook:

Welcome to the Team

Vision of Employer

Structure of Organization

Church Attendance

General Statement about Employees

Ministers

Full Time Staff

Part Time Staff

Volunteers

Proper clothes to wear in the office (covering both sexes)

Salary and Pay Periods

Employee Benefits

Short-Term Disability

Long Term Disability

Social Security/Medicare Tax-Deferred Retirement Program

Medical Insurance

Vision

Dental

Vacation Time

Sick Days or Private Time Off or "PTO" Time and Usage

Family and Medical Leave Act (FMLA)

Vacation days

Vision Coverage

Voting Time

Confidentiality of Work

Employee Evaluations and salary review

Fire Drills

Building Evacuation

Mail

Incoming

Outgoing

Interoffice Mail

Internal Job Posting

Job Descriptions

Jury Duty

Lunch Periods and Cafeteria

Media Relations Policy

Military Leave of Absence

Official Conflict of Interest Policy

Personal Phone Calls

Personal Prayer Requests

Professional Development Program

Resignations

Resolving Conflicts with Co-Workers

Travel Comp Policy

Tuition Reimbursement

Employee Reimbursement

Code of Conduct

Anti-Harassment and Discrimination Policy

Whistleblower Policy

Signed Receipt of Employee Receiving the Handbook

Finally, the handbook must be articulate. If there is any ambiguity, it may favor the employee. Have a local employment law attorney review your policy/procedure manual for compliance with local and state requirements as well as federal laws.

Practice Pointer

Note: Any changes or additions to the Employee handbook should be given to the employee to add in their book, and documented, after they have signed receipt of the new policy. This avoids the argument of not knowing the new policy or procedure.

Annual Evaluation of Staff

The Importance of Employee Evaluations

Over the years, I have found many churches fail in this area. For one reason or another, pastors avoid performing annual evaluations of their staff. I speculate the reasons may be not wanting to confront poor performance, avoiding conflict, being too busy, or not seeing the value of such an exercise.

Here are just a few reasons why performing annual evaluations of your staff is important. First, it forces you to address the work performance in the office and in particular a staff person. Second, it allows the employees to receive feedback on their work performance. Third, it allows the employer to fix performance deficiencies before they get out of hand and/or require termination. Fourth, it gives the employer an opportunity to express undiscovered skills/values unknown to the employee. Finally, it may protect the church in case there are allegations of wrongful termination, discrimination, and the like.

Now that we have discussed the importance of employee evaluations let us now focus on how to do them.

Suggestions on performing employee evaluations:
Be prepared, be honest, be consistent.

Practice Pointer

Prior to the evaluation I give my employee a blank evaluation form and ask them to complete it and bring it with them to the appointment. This helps the employee understand my evaluation criteria. Do not be surprised if the employee honestly reveals their non-strengths. Even if they do not, just the simple act of evaluating themselves has great merit. Some of my past assessment scores (e.g., timeliness, effectiveness, working with coworkers) have been surprisingly similar to my employees' self-evaluations. The form is available from reputable human resource companies.

First, be prepared for the evaluation. Choose the right location to conduct it.

You want it to be a quiet place, professional yet not threatening to the employee. I always preferred my office where I could tell my staff not to interrupt me and prevent phone calls.

Second, be honest in your evaluation. Honest evaluation can be difficult to achieve. This may be based on avoiding conflict or upsetting people. But believe me when I say many people already know their weaknesses. It will not be a surprise to them. Also emphasize their strengths.

Third, be consistent with your evaluations. In other words, treat all employees the same when evaluating them. Do not allow any employee's role or status to influence your assessment. Every position must be judged according to the same criteria. Strive for consistency when scheduling evaluations. I suggest summer or fall, when new budgets are drafted. If the evaluation results in a pay raise, whether by merit or cost of living adjustment (COLA), you have time to implement it with all the employees.

What if the church doesn't do evaluations? Results of no evaluations.

Terminating an employee without proof of poor performance can have its problems. Such an event can result in a lawsuit alleging the termination was a result of a violation of their civil rights not their work performance. The church maintaining an employee file that is full of poor or declining performance evaluations can help rebut such allegations. Second, performing employee evaluations demonstrates management is effectively performing their function to oversee staff seriously. Finally, it can help the church leadership build staff.

Remember you may have an employee you cherish who appreciates the vision and the workplace but who is operating under their potential. Look for that diamond in the rough. There are many people who have great skills who don't realize it and have never been encouraged to advance them in their lives and careers.

Practice Pointer

A couple years ago, my law office received a call from a pastor complaining to me about his secretary whom he was determined to fire. I asked why, and he give me a laundry list of reasons of which several would have been grounds for termination. I asked him how long she had worked at the church, and he said many years. When I asked him to pull her employee file, he said he did not have one, and he never performed an evaluation of her. But then he said, "I am going to this time, and when I do, it will be a doozy. Then I will fire her." I went over the importance of evaluations to establish such patterns of poor behavior to avoid or rebut any legal implications. He did not like what I said. I never heard back from the pastor again. I cannot overemphasize enough the importance of documenting employee performance and properly for termination.

Besides interviewees, prospective hires, and employees, the church leader today has another party to deal with, and that is the "whistleblower." Society has concluded this person performs an important service to the organization and public by reporting when they believe there is evidence of illegal or inappropriate behavior in the church.

What does the church leader do when a whistleblower discloses such information and how should the church respond to the accused and the whistleblower who brought the matter to light?

This is when a properly drafted whistleblower policy comes into play.

Whistleblower Policies and Investigation

A proper whistleblower policy will include all staff, both paid and volunteer. The desire of each entity is to set a standard of business and personal ethics in the conduct of their duties and responsibilities. It requires employees and volunteers to practice honesty and integrity in fulfilling their responsibilities and to comply with all applicable laws and regulations.

In the event an employee or volunteer believes that someone's behavior is in violation of applicable laws, regulations, or any other policy or procedure of the Church, then that individual may file a written complaint with either his or her supervisor or the leadership of the church. It is important to allow the whistleblower to complain to someone else besides their immediate supervisor.

The policy should encourage and enable persons to raise serious concerns within the church prior to seeking resolution outside the church.

In essence, if any employee or volunteer reasonably believes that any policy, practice, or activity of the church is in violation of any applicable law, regulation, policy, or procedure of the church, then they should share their questions, concerns, or complaints with someone who may be able to address them properly. The goal is to resolve the matter internally.

The reporting individual is sometimes uncomfortable speaking with their supervisor or unsatisfied with their supervisor's response. Encourage the reporting individual to speak with another leader or group to receive the complaint.

The reporting individual is not responsible for proving the truth of an allegation. Once they demonstrate reasonable grounds for concern, an investigation begins.

In my practice, I have conducted whistleblower investigations. First, I meet with the complainant to discuss the complaint and its elements. Then, I meet with the alleged transgressor. During this time, I decide whether meeting with a third party is necessary. Once the investigation is complete, I submit a report of my findings and conclusions to the leaders of the church. It is important to investigate the allegations promptly and, if warranted, take appropriate corrective action.

It is also important to keep reports of violations confidential if possible, consistent with the need to conduct an adequate investigation.

Finally, retaliatory measures against complainants are unacceptable. Should retaliation take place, the employer may face a lawsuit.

Employee Discipline

A pastor's most difficult task is to discipline an employee. When an employee needs correction, the easy thing to do is ignore it. But this does not help the employee or the church. The church needs to deal with the problem head on.

I suggest you meet with the employee in your office and go over the issues for the meeting. If the matter is serious, I suggest you lay out the issues in a written evaluation form, stating the facts leading up to the meeting. Then give the employee an opportunity to give his/her side in writing. Finally, you both sign the document before it goes into the employee file. This is important because it creates a paper trail in case there are subsequent events.

Most employee disciplinary actions fall under three categories. First, an **oral warning**. Here, the oral warning is also documented in writing. Second, if another infraction takes place, a **written warning** addressing the previous meeting and the new infraction. Finally, the **final warning**, again in writing, stating the next infraction may result in termination.

All infractions and meetings which address the employee need to be documented to avoid an allegation of wrongful termination.

Dismissing Employees

Terminating an employee is difficult for most people, including leaders. It is often fraught with emotion and pitfalls.

The emotions are clear. You have invested time, money, and support for this team player, and, for whatever reason, the relationship with your ministry must end. Maybe you had high expectations of them? If the members are no longer productive or disrupting the staff, realize others are watching you. As the old saying goes, "hire slow, fire fast."

Ministerial Exception

This important legal principal states courts cannot review employment disputes, relating to both hiring and termination, between churches and their ministers.

The U.S. Supreme court case which established this principal was *Tabor Evangelical Lutheran Church and School v. E.E.O.C.*, 565 U.S. 171 (2012) This significant legal case directly protects the church from court intervention. But who exactly is a "minister"? Courts and attorneys have debated this term arguing if a court should hear such cases. In the past, courts have recognized both pastors and even some teachers who instruct in the Bible to be "ministers". Generally, the closer the employee is to the pulpit in their responsibilities the more likely the church can argue it is protected with the "ministerial exception" protection and the court should not hear the case. It is important to seek the services of an employment attorney to determine the likelihood of a court hearing your church employment dispute.

Pitfalls in Dismissing Employees

One of the pitfalls of dismissing employees is political fallout. Third parties may support or even love the employee more than you. For example, I have had experience when a lead pastor was dismissing an admired staff pastor. Once I had a board member tell me, "I see the staff pastor as my pastor, not the lead pastor. He is my pastor." Such political fallout is common. Others may feel you are terminating an employee simply based on their race or nationality. These objections are common and often based on ignorance of the facts or personal based perceptions of culture. There is little you can do about this because it is often based on emotion. Just realize it is there, and you may have to face it. Do not take it personally.

Secure Legal Counsel Prior to Terminating Employee

I suggest you also seek legal counsel to make sure you are not violating any civil rights, employment agreements, or other legal pitfalls before you meet with the employee and dismiss them. If an employment agreement is in place seek legal counsel on options and recommendations to proceed based on the document. Other legal pitfalls may include various claims of discrimination which the dismissed employee may allege and complain to the EEOC or your State or local Civil Rights Division.

When & where to speak to the employee: Speak with the employee late in the day, versus the morning time. This way, the conversation may be free of interruptions, and you can avoid embarrassment. Have this conversation in the office of the *employee* if they have one. If not, you can meet with the employee in your office. Keep in mind that having this difficult conversation in their office gives the employee a comfortable environment. I found this important since you are initiating the conversation.

The conversation must be direct and honest. Discuss the reasons for the decision and conclude with a discussion about the process. Let them know when their last day is, and if it is immediate, offer them the opportunity to come back the next day after hours to clean out their office. Respect their anticipated embarrassment.

Provide the details of their severance, including Consolidated Omnibus Budget Reconciliation Act (COBRA) information in case they are receiving health care benefits. At this meeting, you may also present a separation agreement for them to consider.

Be careful not to violate the employees' federal, state or local civil rights laws. I strongly encourage consulting with an employment and labor law attorney.

Separation Agreements and Releases.

As a church leader, you should consider using a separation agreement with releases when terminating an employee. This is especially true if you are planning to provide severance for them. There are legal and practical reasons for this.

First, the practical. Why provide money and an agreement to an employee who is resigning or terminating? The reason for such agreements lies in exchange for the financial consideration paid by the church receiving a Release of Claims thus protecting it from a lawsuit.

Second, proper provisions. Since it is an agreement, it must be in writing and signed by both parties to be legally binding; the employee signs off as an agent of the church (employer). Execute the agreement properly and with consideration, ensuring the two parties exchange some value. It may mean compensation or benefits provided by the employer to be received by the departing employee. This consideration validates the agreement. A court may render the agreement legally unenforceable if the parties fail to pay and receive consideration.

Consideration is also given by the employer as an incentive for a release of claims the employee may have against the employer. This is important. You may ask, what claims may a departing employee have against the church? Next, I will review possible federal claims.

Third, and foremost, it should contain a clear waiver or release by the employee of specific or all claims against the church (employer). These claims are a creature of common law, federal and state courts (e.g., violation of Title VII, the Civil Rights Act of 1964). This federal law protects employees from discriminating against them based on color, race, national origin, gender, or religious beliefs. Keep in mind most states also have similar civil rights contained in the state statutes which embodies the common law. Additionally, the employee may be a member of a protected class.

Certain employees, such as those 40 years of age or older, are protected against termination based on their age by the **Age Discrimination in Employment Act or ADEA**. Additionally, this group must be given at least 21 days to consider the agreement, have been given a seven-day revocation period, plus a statement that they have a right to seek the advice of an attorney before signing the agreement. This is important. Employees can waive these protections except the seven-day revocation provision. This cannot be waived.

Fourth, common provisions. Most separation agreements contain certain matters which may be considered. The document may begin with "recital" provisions which outlines the existing relationship between the employer and employee. This may include position held, term of service, compensation he/she receives, and, if necessary, performance reviews. The document will typically include the outgoing compensation the employee will receive, provided he/she agrees to sign the agreement. For example, such a consideration may be six weeks of current pay.

Employers may also include a requirement that the employee not speak to third parties about the agreement nor speak bad about the church or its leadership. They should also agree to resign from all leadership positions both as paid and voluntary roles which may survive the employment. Finally, you may want to have the employees resign their membership. Thus, preventing them from attending any subsequent church membership meeting and using it as a bully pulpit for their grievances.

Language may be included which states a violation of this provision will result in loss of such compensation being paid and even a claw back provision for a violation.

For the above reasons it is imperative you retain a competent nonprofit attorney as well as an employment and labor law attorney to assist the church in drafting this Agreement. I do not suggest finding such a document off the internet.

Once the evaluated employee is terminated and a separation agreement has been signed and executed, the next step is the exit interview.

Exit Interviews

Some organizations perform exit interviews. Exit interviews are when the church interviews the outgoing employee to discuss the process they have experienced leaving and any other matter important to the church. As you can well imagine, this meeting is uncomfortable. However, it can be enlightening. The interviewee is at liberty now, since he/she is no longer employed, to share opinions. I suggest the interviewer be thick skinned and able to receive some hard-hitting comments. I also suggest having the interviewer be a third party who was not their supervisor and present his/her report to the board of directors.

Responding to Reference Checks of Prior Employees

This can be a legal mess if you are not careful. Most past employers who receive a phone call verifying past employment will only verify if he/she worked there and the dates of employment. If the inquirer desires more information, I suggest securing a notarized waiver and release from the previous employee to discuss their past employment.

Should a past employer give damaging information to the inquirer without a Waiver and Release, they may find themselves in a lawsuit by the previous employee. Certain states have a cause of action called "Tortious Interference with a Business Relationship" which allows a party who has suffered a loss of a business interest to sue the party responsible. So, if the church responds negatively to the inquired about a person and that employer does not hire them based on their comments, the aggrieved party may seek damages. Thus, most employers only provide dates of service absent a waiver and release by the prior employee.

So, from interviewing through separation churches face many legal risks when it comes to employment matters. Next, we will speak directly about the other most common and substantial legal risks churches face today.

Action Points for the Next 30 Days:

1. When interviewing prospective hires are you careful to avoid questions which may trigger EEOC violations?
2. If not already, start utilizing Memorandums of Understanding (MOU) to prevent misunderstandings post hiring.
3. Schedule annual employee evaluations.
4. When terminating employees, first make sure you are not violating their civil rights.
5. Set a goal that whenever you're offering severance payment to an employee to secure a separation agreement with a release of all claims against the church. (Remember, including stated paid consideration to the employee is critical).

CHAPTER

8

Legal Risks Facing Churches

Churches face a myriad of risks: association with criminal activities, (embezzlement and theft) and civil torts, (negligence of staff and employees) plus other legal risks regarding property. In this chapter, we will discuss them. Although there are many, I have cited some of the most common I have seen in my practice and grouped them into the following categories: sexual offenses against children, property disputes/embezzlement, and personal injury cases. We will end with discussing the important topic of liability insurance.

An Example of an Embezzlement Issue:

I received a call from a senior pastor who said he had suspicions that his youth pastor was stealing money. The staff member was in charge of the ushers and counters, and he felt uneasy. This senior pastor previously attended a Church Law and Administration class I teach every year to ordination candidates for a state fellowship. In my class where I speak on embezzlement, I suggest conducting what I call the "$100 Bill Test." What you do is deposit a $100 bill in the offering, write down the serial number in case there are other such bills, and see if it makes it in the bank deposit which they usually do.

Resolution of the Issue:

He followed my instructions and discovered it went missing. It was "skimmed." When he approached the youth pastor in charge of offerings about the missing currency, he confessed to the senior pastor to stealing it and later confessed to taking a lot more money. The pastor did not call the police but accepted his resignation. In this example we have a crime of theft and a civil tort of negligent supervision. Occurrences which are crimes are usually glaring but a tort may not be. So, before we continue it would be beneficial if we discussed tort law in general.

Discussion of an Issue: Tort Law in General:

Often, claims made or lawsuits against churches center on a tort. What is a tort? Basically, it is a violation of a **duty of care** imposed by law on a party (here a church) which when **breached causes (causation)** some type of **damages** (economic and noneconomic) to the victim or plaintiff. Thus, the church can be sued by the injured party.

Explanation

Under tort law, the church had a duty to do something but breached that duty at some point which caused an injury or economic damages. A common example is when a minor left in the care of the Youth Pastor who has a duty to protect the minor but fails to do so resulting in harm. For example:

At a church youth event, several youths scooted out for fast food. The youth leaders allowed them to leave. As they crossed the street, a youth was struck by a car and killed. The court determined the church breached its duty of care to protect the minor thus causing the event to take place. Other examples can include slip and fall cases, automobile accident cases, or sexual molestation cases.

Among the many risks churches face, none, in my opinion, are more tragic, expensive, and devastating as child molestation.

#1 Risk: Sexual Offenses Against Minors

The tort of sexual molestation against a minor is a huge risk to churches. As a result, I am often asked about what protections the church should have in place to prevent it and what restrictions, if any, a church should impose on sexual offenders attending the church. Without question, every worker who ministers with children should have a background check done on them. A further measure of checking any references from prior church work would also be beneficial. The formal background check should be done periodically, and the church should contact their liability carrier to seek their recommendation of how often. The background checks should start with the leaders such as the senior pastor and continue down through the rank of volunteers. The leadership should set an example for others to follow.

On the question of allowing convicted sexual offenders or predators to attend, the universal church body has been split on this topic. I find the majority of churches prefer them not to attend while a minority, aware of their presence, allows them provided there are safeguards in place to prevent an occurrence.

Although the court most likely ruled them not to be around children or attend a church service, many ignore such a ruling.

Wording

A brief word about terminology. In this Chapter I am referring to Sexual Offenders in a general sense. The offender may fall into the category of Tier 1, Tier 2, and Tier 3 offender. They can also be convicted as a Sexual "Predator" instead of "Offender" depending on state law, the age of the victim and/or how many times they have committed the offense or being "habitual." So, I am referring to this person as a "sexual offender" in a very general sense.

First, how can you find out if Sexual Offenders (SOs) attend your church?

There are several ways, such as:

- Voluntary disclosure by the offender to the leadership
- Newspaper discloses local SOs.
- Internet SO list, some including pictures, living in your church neighborhood.
- Registration lists of offenders held by police.
- Member of the church or neighbor/public disclosing it.

So, understanding an offender may already be attending your church, what is a church leader to do?

What's a Church Leader to Do?

Recognize Your Risks

These individuals pose a risk to the children on your premises. There is no guarantee they will or will not offend. I categorize it as simply a legal risk if they are present.

Understand the Church is a Public Place

Have you ever thought that sexual predators or molesters can simply walk in with ease? Sure. Churches are places where the public are invited, and they are welcoming. Rightfully so since our desire is to see the lost saved! But keep in mind, such generosity may come at a price. Am I saying we should stop our generous nature? Absolutely not. But I am encouraging a mindset of risk management. Please remember, as I have heard it said, "Risk can never be truly eliminated; it can only be managed." As such, one tool in your toolbox to manage this huge and devastating risk is to come to a decision on the issue of welcoming sexual offenders and then address it in your governing documents.

Recognize the Risk Is Huge

The risk to victims and their family members is huge. A molested child will be affected by such an event for the rest of his/her life. I recently heard on the news the current estimate is one out of three girls, and one out of five boys will be molested. Many years of counseling may be necessary to help them. Abuse may also affect third parties such as their spouse and children. The impact on them is not limited only to the targeted victim but also future family members down the line.

The risk is also huge at the church where the abuse has taken place. Revelation of a child molestation at a church can result in absolute turmoil with the local media coverage investigating the church and its alleged failed safeguards. Such public scrutiny may result in loss of membership and finances. Finally, even after the matter is dealt with, the church may face a stigma for many years to come.

Decide by Policy of the Board and Membership Whether They Can Attend or Not

Churches face a *dilemma*. Do we minister to everyone, and if we do, are we putting our church and most vulnerable members at risk? If we decide to allow them to attend, how can the church minimize this risk?

Many church leaders do not err on the side of grace but prohibit sexual offenders (SOs) from attending their church. But some churches decide to allow SOs to attend with safeguards in place but require them to sign an Attendance Agreement with a chaperone policy. The chaperone will continuously monitor the offender while on the church property.

Such a policy may also become approved by the vote of the leadership and the membership. This way, the church membership agrees with the policy and understands and approves the parameters of attendance or no attendance.

Liability of Church Leadership Allowing SOs to Attend

Allowing offenders to attend is an important legal decision since members of your church board may be found personally liable if a jury finds they acted in gross negligence. Many states offer board members immunity for acts of simple negligence or minor mistakes. But if the decision is "wanton misconduct" or "gross negligence," there could be a loss of statutory immunity. By allowing a sexual offender to attend church knowing their propensity to reoffend, the church may be found guilty of gross negligence if later a child is molested. Gross negligence must be determined in a lawsuit. But being found liable for gross negligence can have a devastating effect since it may award the plaintiff punitive damages which are awarded to punish the church defendant. Punitive damages are extra monetary damages after compensatory damages are awarded to the plaintiff.

Possible Loss of Liability Insurance:

The judgement of punitive damages is extremely serious since the church and the board members may have an exclusion (or no insurance) in the church liability policy for acts of wanton misconduct or gross negligence. In fact, most liability policies I have seen do not cover it. We will discuss liability insurance in more detail at the end of this chapter.

Church liability can also extend to its leaders.

Personal Liability of Directors

Church leaders make many decisions, mostly good but sometimes bad. When this happens a common question is "what liability do I have as a director due to this decision?" Often that depends on the facts, the judgment made, and the subject surrounding it. As a general rule, a director has immunity for decisions or acts of simple negligence. But for this question to be answered correctly in any particular situation, this question must be answered by an attorney in your state who can advise on such matters.

Practice Pointer

Volunteer directors for nonprofits often enjoy personal immunity for acts of simple negligence. Check your own state statutes for such language.

However, I see three exceptions when a volunteer Director's decision may result in personal liability:

1. When a director's decision and/or conduct is criminal in nature; or.
2. When the decision of the Director includes improper personal benefit either directly or indirectly; or
3. The Director makes a reckless decision in bad faith or with malicious purpose or in a manner exhibiting wanton and willful disregard of someone or something.

It is not unusual then for the church's liability insurance company not to extend coverage when these exceptions occur. This is due to the seriousness of the risk. For example, the board approves the hiring of a children's pastor knowing the criminal record check and/or references revealed he is a convicted child molester. Ignoring this they still hire him. Let's assume not long after the hire this individual subsequently reoffends at the church. The jury might not view this hiring decision by the board as simply ordinary negligence but rather as an instance of gross negligence.

Now we will move on to legal issues associated with church property: both real (such as real estate) and personal (money).

#2 Risk: Disputes Relating to the Property of the Church

In the area of property disputes, legal matters come in various ways. So, the following are several common church property disputes I have dealt with in my practice.

Embezzlement:

This theft of church property is not uncommon in the ministry world. Even a cursory review of the newspapers will occasionally reveal theft of money from a church.

Embezzlement is defined in Black's Law Dictionary 8th Edition as "The fraudulent taking of personal property with which one has been entrusted, especially as a fiduciary."[9] In essence, it is the wrongful taking of another's property by one who has been given trust to take care of it.

The act of embezzlement can occur regardless of whether the thief keeps the money or transfers it to a third party. It is also both a crime and civil infraction. The person responsible can be convicted of a crime as well as being civilly sued by the victim (church) for the taking.

Practice Pointer

One morning, I received a call from a pastor who discovered his secretary of many years had been stealing money from the church. She admitted it to him. When I spoke with him about the details of the theft, I discovered she counted the offering, input the contribution, and made the church deposits at the bank. A total absence of internal controls. When the pastor asked her how much she had stolen, she admitted the sum of $30,000. This amount was later discovered to be incorrect. As such, I suggested a forensic audit which revealed $110,000 was stolen. What surprised me was the reason for the theft. She admitted enjoying home shopping tv shows!

Why is embezzlement an issue in our churches?

First, the church is very trusting. Unfortunately, it is sometimes trusting to a fault. Churches are targeted by thieves. Second, where there is money, there are thieves. The church is not exempt from this. It publicly collects money. Cash is placed in baskets or plates passed around and/or deposited in boxes at the back of churches. At one church, a thief dragged the offering box out of the sanctuary to the back of the church yard and broke it open. The offering box contained more than 30 pounds of sand. Third, churches are often institutions dependent on their volunteers, and sometimes this results in a misplaced trust. Note in the definition it says it is the taking of property by someone to whom the property was entrusted. In my experience, the thief is usually a church employee.

9 Bryan Garner, Black's Dictionary: 8th Edition. USA: Thomsen West, 2004, page 561

When I receive a phone call from a church saying they may have an embezzlement issue, my immediate response is sadness which then turns to anger since I understand the hard road this church will now journey upon. I quickly found out in my practice that embezzlement cases come in all shapes and sizes. The thief can be the senior pastor, associate pastor, HR director, church secretary etc., There is no telling. The amount taken can be thousands or hundreds of thousands.

Once the church discovers the theft, there should be several immediate actions. First, remove the thief from doing any further damage. Second, require the thief to disclose how much money was taken, realizing it is probably more than that number. Third, address as a leadership how to deal with this crime.

I have seen it all, but I have found when you boil it down, there are:

Five Truths of Embezzlement

Truth #1: The initially stated amount of money stolen is rarely correct. It is usually more, much more.

In my experience, no thief volunteers the exact sum of money they stole. Most do not even know the total amount they have taken. The reason is usually because the act of stealing becomes a type of drug or addiction. Most of the time the thief guesses, and this should not surprise anyone.

Corollary to Truth #1: The thief is usually also a liar.

Once a person steals money from the church and does not disclose it, they are a liar. Some get convicted and proactively reveal the theft. Others hope they don't get caught. Usually, they are. But not always.

Truth #2: The Church needs to Conduct a Forensic Audit.

What is a forensic audit? Well, first, it is more than just a professional review of finances. It is an in-depth examination of the church's financial records, including transactions to determine if any fraud took place.

This audit may produce evidence for an investigation into the theft. Forensic auditing is a specialization. Most large accounting firms have a forensic auditing department. There are smaller, thus more affordable, accounting firms who do them too.

Paying for an audit helps the leadership fulfill its fiduciary duty to oversee and care for the donations given to the church. This audit is most often used to prosecute a party for fraud, embezzlement, or other financial crimes. If the thief is prosecuted, the accountant conducting the investigation can testify as an expert witness to the results of the forensic audit. But not all embezzlement cases get prosecuted. Over the years representing churches victimized by embezzlement, I have found they usually fall into two groups: those who wish to deal with it in-house and those who desire to have the police involved and the perpetrator prosecuted.

Truth #3: Leadership usually prefers to deal with embezzlement "in-house."

Here, the theft is addressed within the leadership circle without the assistance of law enforcement. This process has its strengths and weaknesses.

The *benefits* of this chosen method are less or no public knowledge of the theft. No public scrutiny of the leadership's failure to properly oversee the finances and/or the employee or volunteer who stole the money. Plus, no questions about how the money was taken, used, or repaid. No scrutiny. Here, the perpetrator can be quietly removed and even required to pay back the money through a confidential agreement. Usually, a church will call me and ask me to draft the agreement for them. The *restitution agreement* is signed by the thief, admitting to the theft, and agreeing to make lump sum or periodic payments to the church to pay back the money. Should the church leadership decide to proceed with this method, I highly suggest securing the services of a professional to draft the agreement. I have done several of these over the years, and my experience is the thief usually makes a few payments and then stops.

There are several *drawbacks* to this approach. First, not reporting a crime may be a crime in and of itself. Remember, with this choice, no one is contacting the authorities, so the thief is not going to be prosecuted for his/her crime. Second, although the matter is being addressed by the leadership it gives an impression of a "cover up." Third, there is no confession to the church body for the theft of their donations. Usually, the board deals with it and then hushes it up. Fourth, a possible violation of a standard of care as stewards of the church's money. The board of directors for a church are fiduciaries. One of their responsibilities is the duty of care to protect and oversee their members' donations. All money received by a nonprofit as donations is held in trust by the board of directors to further the stated nonprofit purpose of the organization. Donations stolen for personal gain violate the corporation's stated purpose to operate as a nonprofit.

Truth #4: The decision to call the police and report the theft is often preferable.

With this choice, the church addresses the matter for what it is: a crime. This choice provides an independent investigation with outside support towards resolution. Upon discovery of the theft, the church notifies the proper law enforcement authorities. Once the pertinent facts are disclosed, the authorities decide if a crime took place and will decide the next steps. Usually, law enforcement officials will collect a statement from the leadership as well as any physical evidence. Additionally, the church may need to cooperate with an internal investigation. The outcome of the investigation will determine whether prosecution is warranted.

There are strengths and weaknesses to this process.

The *strengths* are clear. The assessment has been done by an independent third party. The leadership acted responsibly in protecting the interests of the organization and its property. Following a successful prosecution, the church can then secure a victim's restitution order or court judgment requiring the thief to pay the money back to the church. (With an in-house restitution agreement, the thief is under no court order or judgment to return the church's money.) As the prosecution progresses, the church leadership may disclose the events to the members in a proper setting and update them as the prosecution unfolds.

The *weaknesses* are also evident. The matter is public knowledge. As such, the press may investigate or report on the occurrence. Church employees may need to testify in court, and church members will require detailed information and updates.

On balance, reporting the **theft to authorities** is a proper procedure upon discovery.

Truth Number #5: Determining which stolen money is critical.

You may say, "What does that matter? Money is money." But it does matter. Allow me to explain. The character of money stolen may amplify the problems the church will face. In other words, money stolen from certain accounts may trigger additional liabilities for the church. Here are a few examples to illustrate:

- Were checks stolen out of the church mailbox resulting in a Federal Crime?
- Was money stolen from designated funds? Monies are held in trust for a certain purpose.
- Was the money stolen from escrowed funds to pay payroll taxes? If so, maybe the taxes were never paid, subjecting the church to penalties and interest.

Practice Pointer

A business manager of the church was arrested for embezzlement of church funds. She pled guilty to stealing $82,835 from the church. For five years, she overpaid herself and had the church pay for her health insurance and disability benefit premiums. The church later discovered through a forensic audit another $67,000 was misappropriated in cash donations. Although this is serious money, it is not the end of the story. During her tenure, the business manager failed to make the church payroll tax payments for several years, so the church was liable for $230,000.00 in unpaid taxes, interest, and penalties. The church is currently negotiating with the IRS on these matters. When you add that the church paid $115,000 for attorneys to represent them in negotiations with the IRS, you have an idea of how important it is to determine what money was stolen and its implications.

Suggested Internal Controls to Prevent Embezzlement

Review your internal controls. Internal controls are purposeful actions to prevent improper acts done by others. If your church does not have such internal controls in place allow me to suggest some to avoid embezzlements:

First, have a CPA firm review of church financial records and processes. It is most helpful to have an independent third-party review process. They are professionals who can see weak areas of oversight and make solid recommendations to fix them. You may say "we know what we are doing!" I understand and respect that position; however, allow me to convey an old Chinese saying, "When you're within the frame you do not see the picture."

Second, have a rotating system of ushers and counters to collect and count the offerings. At least two unrelated individuals should receive the church offerings during the worship services and Sunday school. If possible, these individuals should rotate with other individuals in their responsibilities. We consider a married couple as "one." Have a minimum of three people in the room. If possible, have an observer also present who is not a counter.

Third, have a different person(s) record the contribution and make the bank deposit. I fully understand how this may be problematic for smaller churches but do the best you can to split up the duties.

Fourth, now that the money is deposited, it is proper practice for checks to have two signatures above a certain minimum. Online bill payments should also be verified by two people. Keep in mind that a check signer should never sign a blank check.

Even after you have put measures in place to prevent theft, if you find your church is a victim of an embezzler, you need to immediately contact your attorney. Receiving counsel in this situation is critical since the choices the leadership makes right away will have lasting legal and relational impressions on the ministry. Remove the temptation to avoid the situation.

Embezzlement is a serious legal risk churches face.

Another risk churches face is improperly using donated money not for the purpose it was given. In church we call it the act of "converting."

Converting Restricted Donations Towards Operating Expenses

Here we will discuss the legal risk of taking contributions (churches property) received for a specific purpose but spending it another way. This issue usually comes up when a church finds its operating account is low and the pastor and/or board decides to transfer money from a donor restricted account to make up for a short fall in the operating account.

The environment conducive for this is when there is a downturn in the economy and the pastor and board see the operating fund balance dropping due to less giving. Most for-profit businesses will act quickly and reduce expenses to offset the loss of revenue. But in the church world, this is often resisted. At times, church leadership will not cut staff, which is usually one of their largest expenses, for "loss of faith" or appearance.

When in crisis, the board may see no reason why it cannot simply vote to transfer designated funds to the operating account and correct the short fall. If you have served on a board, you may have experienced this. Church leaders need to be careful doing this without legal counsel.

The Mississippi Supreme Court in 2009 stated the following in its holding: *"The general law of contributions has been stated to be: 'Where a religious society raises a fund by subscription for a particular purpose, it cannot divert the funds to another purpose, and, if it abandons such purpose, the donors may reclaim their contributions'.*"[10]

Court cases such as these may support allegations of a *breach of trust.*

This can happen when board members authorize the diversion of designated funds from their intended purposes or projects. This is based on the premise that when a church raises money for a project it holds those funds in a *constructive trust* until the project is paid and/or completed. If the money is spent for other reasons a breach of trust may be alleged and damages sought.

Who is responsible for such actions? Church directors and officers may be legally accountable for violating the terms or restrictions of properties and funds held in trust by the church.

Who has standing to file the lawsuit?

Keep in mind this assumes the **complainant has** the legal right or "standing" to enforce the original designation. Not everyone can come forward and sue. Usually this is restricted to those who are donors or their legal representatives.

What if the donor is deceased?

In cases where the original donor or family member can't enforce it, the "aggrieved party" may be able to file a complaint with the state attorney general, who may then force the provisions of the constructive trust. The laws on this vary from state to state. An aggrieved party may be a beneficiary of the estate or even a church member who wanted the gift to be used for its intended purpose. Either way, the affected party may go to court and/or notify the state attorney general. This risk usually occurs when the church leadership is not responsive to the aggrieved party.

Unwinding the Conversion of Funds

If you find your church in this dilemma, I suggest you seek legal counsel and a CPA for a solution. As a general rule, I suggest you first contact the original donor and request release of the restricted designated purpose. Explain the situation to the donor and have him or her sign an authorization to release the restriction,

10 *Schmidt v. Catholic Diocese* of Biloxi 18 So3d 814 (Miss. 2009).

thereby authorizing the gift, in whole or part, to be transferred to the general fund for general purposes.

If the donor does not agree, then you will have to continue honoring the designated and restricted purpose or return the donation. Returning the donation may have further complications since it will require the church to change its financial reporting and the donor may have to file an amended tax return because the church probably gave the donor contribution credit for the donation, thus my suggestion to engage a CPA to help guide the parties.

Guidance can often be found in your state law. Many states have statutes and case law explaining to the church what it must do in such circumstances.

One such law is the Uniform Prudent Management of Institutional Funds Act of 2006 (UPMIFA) which has been adopted, as of this publication, in 47 states. UPMIFA gives clear guidelines to release and modify such restrictions on charitable funds. This law was drafted by the National Conference of Commissioners on Uniform State Laws (NCCUSL). The Act states its goal is to "provide states with non-partisan, well-conceived and well-drafted legislation that brings clarity and stability to critical areas of state statutory law." UPMIFA provides a number of options for modifying or releasing the restrictions on such funds. The church should consult with an attorney to see if their state has adopted this Act and give leadership legal guidance to modify or release the funds.

Observations on the legal risk of Conversion:

First, recognize that donated money received for a specific purpose may be held in a "constructive trust" to be honored by the church leadership.

Second, the board of directors' action to convert said money may not be legal. It requires the restriction to be lifted by the donor, not the Board. I suggest you receive such authorization in writing signed by the donor. If the donor wants the donation returned to him/her, inform the donor if the church does return the gift the donor may have to file an amended tax return.

Illustration of Special Membership Meeting to Resolve the Issue

I once assisted a senior pastor who needed $70,000 for an operating account. He informed me the board wanted to simply move and approve the conversion without speaking with the donors. The pastor asked them to wait until he had spoken with me about the situation. I suggested the board call for a Special Membership Meeting, where the pastor could explain the current financial position and ask the donors who gave to the building fund to release the restriction on the gifts. I also advised him to distribute cards on which donors could identify themselves, record the amount of their donation, and authorize releasing the restriction (i.e., in whole or part) to help the church. Many released the restriction, and more than $70,000 went into the operating account to stabilize the church's finances. The pastor gave assurance to those donors who did not release their donation, again thanking them for their donation, that their restriction would continue to be honored and used as promised. Resolving this matter brought the pastor and the board great relief. No one asked for the return of their donation. Due to the leadership's transparency, tithes and offerings increased each Sunday.

Third, failure to follow the law in your state may result in a lawsuit against the church for breach of trust. Action for breach of trust is usually filed by the original donor or his/her personal representative who has "standing" to bring the suit against the church. Black's Law Dictionary (8th Edition) defines "standing" as "A party's right to make a legal claim or seek judicial enforcement of a duty or right."[11]

Fourth, unilateral action without the donor's permission to convert the funds may tarnish the credibility of the church leadership. This may result in diminished ability to receive donations when requested. Consult with local legal counsel and a CPA for clear direction before taking any action.

Practice Pointer

Offering Envelopes with Broad Discretion/Disclaimer

Church leadership tries to avoid these legal issues by writing a disclaimer on the offering envelope giving broad discretion to the board on use of any donations:

"Our church will make every effort to honor the contribution designation of the donor. But since all contributions become the property of the church, we reserve discretion to determine what is the best use of the gift."

I can understand the desire for such discretion, but does it legally lift the restriction, especially when the money is clearly requested and then received for a designated purpose? Often, I have seen churches ask for a

11 Bryan Garner, Black's Dictionary: 8th Edition, pg. 1442

designated gift and then ask the people to use these envelopes with the disclaimer language printed on it. The fact that the money is placed in an envelope with language stating otherwise, in my opinion, may not release the church to use the money for reasons other than the stated purpose. The donor may allege the use of an envelope does not remove the constructive trust connected with the gift.

Another major legal risk to churches involves their real property and its use. The following section discusses property zoning matters.

In addition to legal risks, church property also raises issues regarding zoning and usage.

#3 Risk: Property Zoning and Usage Matters

Another major legal risk to churches involves use of their real property.

Leasing Unused Building Space

Most churches who hold title to real property have requested or obtained an exemption from Ad Valorum or property taxes. As such, they have notified their county property appraiser or tax collector office they intend to use the property exclusively for religious purposes. Then, if approved, no real estate taxes apply. It will be designated as "exempt."

Legal disputes in this area focus on when the church uses the exempt property for commercial purposes instead of religious purposes. This can happen when the church enters a lease with a for-profit entity to use their exempt property.

It is such a temptation to lease unused building space and receive that monthly rent check. Usually there is no problem with such a transaction if both parties are nonprofits and share a common belief system. However, trouble rears its head when the arrangement is between a nonprofit and a *for*-profit corporation. I have encountered several similar transactions.

In my experience, churches fall into this risk more when there is a dip in the economy and in offerings, so they become aggressive, seeking funding from sources other than donations.

Leasing Church Property to a For-Profit Business such as Food Trucks.

Here we will be discussing more than an occasional visit by a food truck, however, even then the church needs to be careful. This issue often occurs when a pastor encounters a "generous businessman" who, in exchange for using the parking lot to sell food, generously tithes on the revenue or donates to the church from the sales. It all seems innocent enough. The church or school employees benefit from the easy purchase of food, and in turn, the church or school benefits from the additional revenue. Sometimes, however, the church or school gets hurt.

Such arrangements may seem harmless. However, they may place your real property tax exemption and/or exemption with the IRS in jeopardy.

The issue centers on the improper use of the church or school property. Under many state zoning laws, churches and nonprofit schools are exempt from paying property taxes since their primary or exclusive purpose is to operate in a religious nonprofit fashion. When the nonprofit entity operates in a commercial fashion such as selling food and receiving revenue from such sales, it no longer operates exclusively in a nonprofit fashion. This becomes clearer when the food truck is a for-profit business. The property may no longer be used *exclusively* or *predominantly* for religious purposes. To remain exempt from paying property taxes, the entity must operate consistently with their core, religious purposes, or other exempt purposes. Local legal counsel can guide you on the state law and its wording as it relates to usage. Straying outside these protections runs the risk of losing your exemption (whole or part) and being liable for back property taxes during the time you operated commercially.

Coffee Shops

This issue also comes up when a pastor calls my office about starting a coffee shop. Churches need to be careful about how it opens a coffee shop whether it is inside the church or a standalone venture. This is illustrated in Private Letter Ruling 201645017 which is included in the books (See Appendix 2). Here the IRS determined *"Specifically, the facts show you are not operated exclusively for section 501©(3) purposes because a substantial portion of your activities consists of the operation of a coffee shop in a commercial manner."* In addition, a church needs to be aware of issues related to the Unrelated Business Income Tax (UBIT) and/or state sales tax which may become due from coffee sales.

Church Defense:

The church could argue "incidental use" on the church property, claiming the church property can still be used exclusively or predominantly for religious purposes since the commercial activity (i.e., food truck) is incidental or de-minimums. For example, Florida Law states under Florida Statute 196.196 (2)

(emphasis is mine)

"Only those portions of property ***used predominantly*** *for charitable, religious, scientific, or literary purposes are exempt. The portions of property which are* ***not predominantly used*** *for charitable, religious, scientific, or literary purposes are not exempt. An exemption for the portions of property used for charitable, religious, scientific, or literary purposes is not affected so long as* ***the predominant use*** *of such property is for charitable, religious, scientific, or literary purposes. In no event shall an* ***incidental use*** *of property either qualify such property for an exemption or impair the exemption of an otherwise exempt property."*

Keep in mind what constitutes "incidental use" is a matter of available case law, statutory definition and/ or county or court interpretation.

Allowing a for-profit business to lease or use space is complicated and may result in losing some or all property tax exemption. Further, as the next Case in Point illustrates, the church may owe back property taxes.

Case in Point

A church pastor is approached by a for- profit Christian School to lease unused building space during the week. The school promises not to use the church property on Wednesday night or over the weekend. This way it does not interfere with their church services. The school agrees to pay $1,500 a week in rent and presents a lease for signature. Since Covid-19 hit, attendance has been down, as well as offerings. The pastor is pleased having a Christian School with a Christian name on their premises and feels this is good stewardship of their property. The pastor approached the board and after much discussion agreed to sign the lease. It is unknown if the board and pastor sought legal or accounting advice on the matter.

A few years pass and the county, during a routine inspection, discovers this arrangement. The appraiser's office deemed that the church violated its religious exemption status and issued a tax lien in the total of $475,000.00 that includes interest and fines for the years going back to when the lease was initially signed. The reason for the owed taxes was because the school was not a non-profit but an LLC or "for-profit" entity. Since the property was supposed to be used "exclusively" for religious purposes, the presence of the school violated the law. In other words, the church was involved in a commercial, not a religious, transaction. The church is challenging the back taxes and fines owed to the county.

Formula for Calculation of County Property Taxes Owed

Some state statutes provide a formula to calculate the exempt space used by the for-profit to determine the amount of back taxes the church owes. Keep in mind that the taxing authorities may calculate it retroactively to the date of the initial lease. This can mean tens of thousands of dollars owed by the church.

Failure to Receive Sales Tax for Leased Property

Another legal risk may arise from not paying sales tax. When a nonprofit leases its property to another nonprofit both parties are usually exempt from paying state sales taxes. Thus, they do not collect it. However, for-profit corporations are generally not exempt from paying sales taxes on leased property. In this case, the nonprofit church collecting the rent payment from a for-profit entity may not collect the required sales tax, thus failing to pay the state the taxes owed. This can place the church at legal risk of noncompliance with the state taxing authorities.

The lesson here is clear. It is important for churches who are considering such transactions to seek professional counsel before entering into them. As a general rule, only property that is predominantly or exclusively, used for "charitable, religious, scientific or literary purposes," language of the IRS, may be deemed exempt from real property taxation.

Proper Discovery on the Identification of Leasing Party:

Be careful *not* to assume a religiously named organization is a nonprofit. I have seen many Christian-named businesses sound like a nonprofit only to discover through my investigation they were in fact a for-profit corporation or a limited liability company (LLC). Don't take their word for it and conduct due diligence.

Suggestion:

If the lessee is a non-church entity (i.e., school or club) and they are claiming to be an exempt nonprofit, then request a copy of their IRS Letter of Determination to validate their exempt status.

Practice Pointer

One afternoon a church called the office about being approached by a small elementary school to hold classes on their property. I asked if they were an exempt entity, and the church said they were. When I encouraged the church to verify this by requesting the schools Letter of Determination from the IRS, they assured me it was not necessary since they were a Christian school. I offered to make the request for the church and received a verbal verification, but no Determination Letter was ever received. I discovered they were an out-of-state Christian for-profit entity doing business in Florida. The church decided against entering into a lease agreement with the school.

Additional Legal Risks Nonprofits May Face Leasing Space to Outside Groups:

Receiving Revenue and Unrelated Business Income Tax IRS FORM 990T

This tax form may be required due to income received from leasing church property. This may be due to the fact the income is not a donation. It is important to seek the counsel of a CPA to verify whether FORM 990T must be filed.

Possible Violation of Public Accommodation Laws

Leasing church property to another nonprofit (Christian School) may "open the door" to leasing space to another nonprofit which may not follow your church's religious purposes. When a church leases space, it may argue it is entering into a "commercial" not a religious transaction and as such must follow public accommodation laws. It raises the question: can the church then refuse leasing to a different entity for wanting the similar space too? Note: some state and municipal codes offer exemption to churches in the area of public accommodation. If you're not sure, consult with a religious constitutional law organization.

Personal and/or Emotional Injury Claims

Churches have these risks, but leasing space out to another group is a multiplier of these risks. You have more people on the church property conducting more activities.

Thus, more opportunities for unfortunate or tragic events. Let's next take a look the legal risks of personal injuries.

Risk #4: Personal Injury Cases

Personal injury cases come in many shapes and sizes. They can come about through a slip and fall, a church van having an auto accident, or negligence by church employees. Here, I will address several of the most common personal injury cases involving churches and liability insurance.

Personal Injury Caused by Vehicular Accidents

A common legal risk churches face is automobile accidents by negligent church drivers. There are myriad opportunities for this to happen, including youth trips, picking up kids for church, and out-of-the-area church functions and events. One of the more common legal questions I receive in the personal injury risk area is when a pastor calls and says their church van was in an auto accident. What do they do? I first make sure all the parties involved have received proper medical attention. Then I focus on inquiring about the church's commercial auto *bodily injury liability policy.* It is common for a church to have auto and general liability coverage of at least $1,000,000. per event. Such coverage offers protection in case the church is sued.

One type of automobile insurance often overlooked is *uninsured and underinsured coverage.* This will protect the church if an accident involves an uninsured or underinsured driver. With this type of insurance, your carrier will settle these claims with you directly versus the other driver's insurance carrier.

Insuring for liability is key to the church for any negligence its volunteers or employees commit. Many plaintiffs' attorneys representing auto accident victims look to sue at least two parties. Who are they? First, the driver of the vehicle who allegedly negligently caused the accident. Second, the owner of the vehicle who allowed the driver to drive the vehicle.

Should the church find itself involved in an auto accident, I would suggest the following: First, make sure all the injured parties are seeking and receiving medical attention. Second, notify your insurance agent and carrier of the accident. The adjuster for the church's liability carrier will most likely request a recorded statement of events.

Going forward, the insurance policy may require the church to cooperate with the insurance company as it investigates, negotiates a settlement, and prepares a trial defense. This does not necessarily mean you are legally obligated to cooperate with the opposing party's insurance company or lawyer. The church's insurance defense attorney can guide you. Your contract with the insurance company is your policy. Its provisions guide the church (insured's) and insurance company's (insurer's) obligations.

What would the plaintiff or injured party allege? Most likely some form of the following: the church owned the vehicle and had a duty of care to the passengers in the vehicle or other parties, permitting a driver to operate it, who then operated the vehicle negligently which caused an accident which injured and/or caused economic and non-economic damages to the claimant. Although many parties settle privately, some cases make it to court.

In most cases, churches with liability insurance will receive legal defense counsel from the carrier, including representation and guidance through the court processes.

Practice Pointer

Maintaining a commercial automobile liability policy is extremely valuable. Most policies will cover the church for claims of one million dollars or more. Obviously, the higher the coverage the more protection to the church. The policy limits will most likely cover any judgment up to the stated amount. Many overlook the paid coverage of attorney fees for defense by the insurance company. This is extremely valuable since they usually hire excellent defense attorneys to represent their insureds.

Premises Liability

These are lawsuits brought by individuals who were injured while on the church property. Although events such as the after-hours martial arts class are rare, the more common lawsuits involve slips and falls. It is common for a church visitor or member to break their ankle in a pothole on the property or slip in a puddle by a doorway.

With premises liability, it is important to discuss the required elements of such a case. To successfully have a premises liability case usually there are four legal elements which must be satisfied. First, establishing the "duty of care" owed by the property owner. Second, proving the owner "breached" that duty of care by failing to maintain the premises properly or warn of a known danger. Third, the owner's negligence in doing so directly caused the harm. Finally, the result was some physical injury and/or economic damages.

Illustration of Personal Injury on Church Property Caused by Third Parties

A pastor welcomed a taekwondo teacher to use the church property to conduct classes. The pastor felt it was a good idea since it would keep the kids "off the streets." The teacher used the church property after hours and had access to the whole building they met in. The church promoted his class as a ministry of outreach to the community. After class one day, the teacher sexually assaulted a student. The police and newspapers were involved so the church went through a terrible ordeal. Fortunately, no lawsuit was filed against the church.

Church Liability centers on the duty of care it owes to the injured party. The duty of care owed by the church to them mainly depends on their designation. The church does not owe each visitor the same duty of care. As such, it is important to understand why that person was on the church property. Were they there to attend church? Drop off some package? Maybe they decided to enter the church property to conduct mischief?

There are generally three types of people who walk on the church property: trespassers, licensees, and invitees. **The standard of care by the church for each of these people is different so let's look at them.**

Trespassers are defined in Black's Law Dictionary 8th Edition as "One who commits trespass; one who intentionally and without consent or privilege enters another's property."[12] The church owes the least duty to unforeseeable **trespassers.** This is why churches are generally encouraged to post "No Trespassing" signs on playgrounds and sports areas.

Licensees are defined in Black's Law Dictionary 8th Edition as "One who has permission to enter or use another's premises, but only for one's own purposes and not for the occupier's benefit."[13] An example may be a door-to-door salesperson who visits to sell a product. The church generally has a duty to warn licensees of any dangerous conditions known to the church but unknown to the licensee.

12 Garner, Black's Law Dictionary, 8th Edition, Page 1543

13 Garner, Black's Law Dictionary, 8th Edition, Page 939

Invitees are defined in Black's Law Dictionary 8th Edition as "A person who has an express or implied invitation to enter or use another's premises such as a business visitor or a member of the public to whom the premises are held open."[14] In the church world this may be your members, adherents, invited visitors and guests attending or visiting the church. Property owners owe the highest duty to **guests and invitees**. When it comes to the invitee, the church has a clear duty to inspect the premises and warn the invitee of any dangerous conditions on the property.

Practice Pointer

The church must give the most care to those invited. Why? Because the church has a duty to inspect and maintain the property so there are no hazards which can injure them. For example, Vicki, a long-standing member, drives to the church and trips in a pothole while exiting the car. The church parking lot and its potholes have been a topic of discussion with the church board for many months, but they did not address repairing them nor post any signs to prevent injury. The church has a duty to maintain a safe parking lot, and it failed in that duty which allegedly resulted in her injury. Vicki decides to sue the church because she has $20,000 in medical bills for her broken ankle. The church must inspect and maintain the church property and fix any known hazards.

Besides premises liability, churches are also vulnerable to negligent actions by volunteers and employees. This can include negligent supervision of employees and volunteers as well as negligent hiring.

Negligent Selection or Hiring.

Employers are legally responsible for the negligent acts of their employees and volunteers. This legal doctrine is called "respondent superior." This term has the Latin meaning "let the superior make answer." Blacks further defines it as "The doctrine holding an employer or principal liable for the employees' or agent's wrongful acts committed within the scope of the employment or agency."[15] This is a very broad risk which covers many activities.

The church may also be responsible for negligent acts of its volunteers.

14 Garner, Black's Law Dictionary, 8th Edition, Page 846

15 Garner, Black's Law Dictionary, 8th Edition, Page 1338

Case in Point

A live video feed of the church service is wired into the nursery for the workers to see and hear while they are taking care of the children. Every day, a video of the room and its activities are kept for security reasons. One day, a tragedy occurs, and the video tape is reviewed. It revealed a worker in a rocking chair watching the church service while rocking a newborn to sleep. However, due to the growth of the church, the workers brought in a few toddlers into the nursery room. While the worker was rocking the chair, a toddler's arm was caught under the rocker. As she rocked, one can see her severely injuring a toddler's arm. With the noise of the children and the service, she did not realize right away what was happening. The physicians had to amputate the child's arm. An allegation of negligent supervision was made against the church for improperly mixing the age groups of the children and negligently supervising the part-time employee / worker who caused severe personal injuries to the toddler. The church's liability carrier settled the case.

In summary, churches face legal risks on a daily basis. Sexual molestation of minors, auto accidents, premises liability, risk of loss of property tax exemption, embezzlement, converting designated offerings, personal injuries and more. Keep in mind, no church leader can eliminate all risks, but they can work to reduce or mitigate them.

Finally, securing liability insurance to protect the church is critical should an event happen.

Now let us discuss liability insurance in detail. We will look at the types of coverage available to churches. Then we will address how the different types of policies apply to legal events which commonly occur at churches. We will wrap up with the Insurance Carrier claiming "Reservation of Rights" and how this affects the church's liability exposure.

Church Liability Insurance Coverage

The current U.S. insurance market is difficult at best. Churches are being dropped and others due to premium increases are shopping around. Some Insurance companies are leaving certain states and are no longer writing policies there. But the need to secure adequate liability coverage and having the correct coverage is critical. What insurance should I consider for my church? Here are some suggestions:

General Liability Insurance

Commercial Auto Insurance

Building Insurance

Directors and Officers (D&O) Liability Insurance

Professional Liability Insurance for counseling and pastoral care

Special Event Insurance

Cyber Security Insurance

Employment Practices Liability Insurance

Workers' Compensation

Abuse and Molestation

Some insurance companies used to cover child sexual abuse claims within the limits contained in general liability policies. As the song goes: *those days are gone.* This risk often requires a special rider which not all carriers offer. Several insurance carriers offer riders and additional coverages for this risk, meaning it is an extra premium over and above the cost for general liability coverage.

Such additional coverages for sexual molestation and the like can be noted in policies as: sexual abuse, sexual harassment, inappropriate sexual relationships, child molestation, peer sexual abuse, sexual assault, and the like. Discuss available options with your insurance agent to ensure your church is properly insured.

It is also important to discuss how liability insurance policies work.

In keeping with the current significant legal risk topic, our working example will be liability claims associated with sexual molestation of a minor.

The following sections examine two main types of insurance policies.

"Claims Made" Liability Insurance Policies

These policies protect the church against allegations of sexual abuse that are properly reported and occur after the policy start date. Once a claim is known, your policy or contract with the insurance company will require a timely notification to them once the insured or the church learns of the event. Failure to do so may result in a "reservation of rights" letter to the detriment of the church.

For example, assume the church liability policy begins January 1, 2021, and ends December 31, 2021. During a children's church event on March 1, 2021, a child was sexually abused. The church learns of the allegation by an attorney letter received on June 30, 2021. Immediately the church notifies the insurance agent and company on July 1, 2021. Since the church has a claims made liability policy covering this event *and* because the claim was timely reported during the policy period, the church has insurance coverage under the policy.

However, sometimes the church learns of abuse years later. What coverage does the church have then? Assuming under the above facts the abuse took place in 2017 but was reported to the church by the attorney letter received on June 30, 2021, does the current liability policy cover the church? No, it does not. The 2017 sexual abuse incident will not be covered with the 2021 claims made policy because the abuse occurrence and report did not occur within the policy period of January 1-December 31, 2021.

Since many abuse claims come forward years later the church has another option: "occurrence" based policies.

"Occurrence" Liability Insurance Policies

This type of insurance policy covers abuse incidents that occur during a specific policy period. This holds true regardless of when the allegation is reported to the insurance company. The notification could take place a few years after the event. Allow me to remind the reader of the obligation to immediately report the claim. The following may illustrate my point.

Assume the church liability policy continuing with child abuse coverage has been purchased on an occurrence basis year after year since January 1, 2017. The current policy is in effect on January 1, 2021, and ends on December 31, 2021. During a children's church event a child was sexually abused on March 1, 2018. The church received a letter from a plaintiff's attorney about the allegation on June 30, 2021, three years later. Immediately, the church notifies the insurance agent and company on July 1, 2021. Since the church has an "occurrence policy," had an active policy covering this risk at the time of the abuse, and the claim was promptly reported the church has coverage. This is true even though the abuse took place three years earlier during a previous effective policy period. This is the benefit of the occurrence type insurance policies. Annual renewing of this policy is critical for coverage.

Practice Pointer

I have recently learned at least one insurance company, while promoting their coverage on their Sexual Abuse and Molestation Coverage, said it is available to be added on a stand-alone claims-made policy. Then they said they can also add this coverage to a combined general liability policy as an endorsement to an occurrence form policy. But either way, apparently the coverage provided is included as "claims-made" coverage. This way all coverages are written apparently under a single policy.

This is interesting. Contact your agent as there are options for churches.

Duty to Defend the Church

One of the major benefits of having liability insurance is having legal defense paid for by the carrier. This benefit is purely contractual. Remember the policy is a contract between the church and the insurance company. There is no common law obligation to defend the church. Keep in mind, in most of the liability insurance policies I have dealt with, the duty to defend will end when the applicable limits of insurance are exhausted, due either to a court judgment or settlement. It is important for the church leader to understand this because in a serious case where the liabilities may exceed the policy limits, and/or the attorney's fees would be substantial, the insurance company may decide to tender the limits and try to get out of the obligation to pay for further legal defense. If the church's liability limits are low, this can be an issue. But the insurance carrier must be careful as you will see next.

Good Faith or Bad Faith?

The insurer has a duty to act in "good faith" by properly handling the claim and not simply "tendering the limits" and then terminating its obligation to defend. In all matters between the insured (church) and the insurer (liability carrier), it is the insurance company who must act in "good faith." In other words, as ruled. "*Where, as here, the policy limits are much lower than the insured's potential exposure, the insurer cannot put its own interests first, but must negotiate as it would if its liability limits were unbounded.*"[16] This Federal District Court of appeals citing another case they also ruled on earlier with even clearer language stating: *"the duty to negotiate in good*

16 **Peckham v. Continental Cas. Ins. Co.,** 895 F.2d 830, 834-35 (1st Cir. 1990).

faith would require the carrier to give 'the interest of the insured' consideration 'equal to that consideration given its own interest,' or 'to treat the claim as if it were alone liable for the entire amount'."[17] As stated, the insurance carrier must place the interests of the church equally with theirs.

There are occasions, regardless of policy limits, when although the church has the needed liability insurance the carrier may not cover all or some of the claim. Often this occurs when the church leader fails to act promptly to a claim and when that happens the insurance company may send a letter indicating the insurance carrier may not cover the full claim. Remember my example of the new pastor finding a served lawsuit in the previous pastor's desk?

Reservation of Rights Letter.

This letter from the insurance company agrees to defend you or your church under a "reservation of rights," meaning if the church is sued, the insurance company will reluctantly agree to defend the church/policyholder as the insurance policy requires for now but may not later. Why? Because if the insured fails to notify the claim timely, it may jeopardize the insurance carrier's ability to adjust the claim properly. So, the insurance company reserves the right to later deny coverage since the terms of the policy were not followed.

Why do insurance companies send these letters out when they can just deny coverage? Good question. The answer lies in four words insurance companies do not want to hear. An allegation they are "acting in bad faith." Remember that? Basically, each insurance policy requires the insurance company in exchange for receiving the church premiums to do two things. First, defend the insured church on the claim and second, indemnify the insured for any judgement up to the policy limits contained in the policy. Insurance carriers don't wait to send out this letter in order to protect their rights and also to prevent an allegation of "bad faith" towards their insured, the church.

Acting in bad faith could result in a civil claim against the insurance company. Each state has laws on this cause of action. They can be both common (court rulings) and/or statutory laws on bad faith. In essence, it means the church insured may bring a civil action against the insurance company when the carrier is not attempting in good faith to settle claims when, under all the circumstances, it could and

17 **Voccio v. Reliance Ins. Cos.,** 703 F.2d 1, 2 (1st Cir. 1983)

should have done so. So, the insurance carrier needs to know immediately when a claim is brought forth so it can comply with this standard of practice. The church's attempt to hide or delay the conveyance of this claim to their insurance carrier may result in jeopardizing its resolution and/or costing the insurance company more to adjust the claim.

The insurer may state it is reserving its right to deny coverage for all or part of the claim if, after further investigation, it determines that the claim is not covered under the language in the policy.

Practice Pointer

One day, my office received a phone call from a board member stating his concern that the pastor had received a letter the previous month from an attorney representing a minor who was allegedly sexually assaulted during a church youth event. The board member said the pastor called for the leadership to pray and seek God, asking him to remove this "attack on his church." No response was given to the plaintiff's attorney, and no notification was made to the church liability insurance carrier. The church leaders just prayed about the matter. After 60 days, the church was served a lawsuit for the event, and then the church called the insurance company wanting an attorney to represent them. The insurance carrier assigned a law firm to represent them but also sent a reservation of rights letter to the church due to the delay of reporting the allegations/claim and the likely resulting loss of coverage under the policy. Similar language as the following was provided to the church:

"This letter is to serve as a reservation of "insurance company's" rights to deny coverage and/or defense under the policy and/or applicable law and further, with respect to defense costs incurred or to be incurred in the future, to be reimbursed and/or obtain an allocation of attorney's fees and expenses if it is determined that there is no coverage."

Prompt written notification is critical to ensure the liability insurance is active and the insurance company has timely notice to investigate the claim and will not hold the church responsible for attorney fees and costs of the claim. In other words, pray about the matter along with following the policy and notifying the liability carrier.

Food for Thought

Suggestions should your church receive a Reservation of Rights letter:

First, if you know the reasons for the letter, pull the policy and review it to determine if the carrier is correct.

Second, if you do not understand why the letter was sent, request the reasons for it.

Third, importantly, immediately consult with your church attorney to advise on the implications of the letter and seek legal advice to move forward.

By understanding the letter and its implications, the church leader can better prepare and protect the interest of the church and its membership.

Important Suggestion

In my opinion, church leadership must engage an insurance professional that has experience in this marketplace with church liability insurance. Today's church leader cannot simply rely on someone that may have an insurance license but is only casually engaged in the church insurance industry. The financial security of the ministry could be at risk if they do not partner with a trusted advisor when purchasing the correct insurance coverage for your ministry.

Now, let's move away from legal risks and liability insurance to the topic of various real estate transactions and the church.

Action Points for the Next 30 Days:

1. Adequately screen all volunteers and employees working with minors.
2. Verify your church has internal financial controls in place to prevent theft or embezzlement.
3. If your church is leasing any real property, verify it is with another nonprofit and not a for-profit entity.
4. Have your trusted church insurance agent verify proper coverages, such as directors' liability, acts of negligence, sexual offenses against minors, in the church liability insurance policy.

5. If the church is missing important coverage(s) request a premium quote to include them and make provision for them in your budget.

CHAPTER

9

Real Estate: Leasing, Purchasing and Closing

Is your church in need of more space? Then you may need to consider expanding your stakes! In this chapter, we will discuss a topic often overlooked for churches and nonprofits: leasing and purchasing real property. I believe there are primarily two reasons for this oversight.

First, the real estate needs of nonprofits vary: lease or purchase? Should a ministry buy raw land and build, expand on existing property, or simply lease commercial space? Church needs vary because of its size and available land or space in its location.

Second, the laws that impact purchasing real estate vary from state to state. Since the laws, ordinances, and zoning designations are very local, I will speak in general terms; however, as with all legal matters, it is important to consult with a local real estate attorney in your community prior to executing a lease or contract for purchase or sale of real property.

An Example of the Need to Purchase Real Property:

A senior pastor asked me to review his master plan for his church. A master plan is a dynamic, long-term planning document which provides a conceptual layout to guide future growth and development. It is a visual document which makes a connection between buildings, social settings, and their surrounding environments. It represents the ultimate "build out" of the property.

Resolution of the Issue:

I discovered the architect included parcels of land not owned by the church. When I questioned the architect about it, he didn't realize his mistake. The plan was useless unless the church purchased the neighbor's land. I suggested we go to prayer and then approach the property owners about buying the property. Within a few years, the church had purchased nearly all the necessary land.

Discussion of the Issue: Going alone or secure professional assistance?

How do you start? You have a choice: secure realtor assistance or do the leg work yourself.

1. **Realtor Assistance**

   A great benefit for the church is securing the assistance of a professional realtor. They have the knowledge and experience of the local market and can assist you through the process. Additionally, the seller usually pays the realtor's commission for the transaction. This is true with both leases and purchasing. So, the church can acquire professional help, and their professional connections, at no direct cost.

   Who should you choose? Allow me to first suggest the assistance of a locally licensed REALTOR®. They are a professional trade organization of more than 1,500,000 agents who subscribe to a strict code of ethics. Local professionals have a "boots on the ground" knowledge and experience. Check their credentials and level of experience to see if it matches your expectations.

   Many of today's realtors are also transaction agents. This allows them to facilitate between buyer and sellers while closing transactions. They have no fiduciary duty to protect the church's interests. However, a realtor acting as a buyer's agent represent the interests of the buyer (e.g., the church) and no one else.

The realtor can assist in several specific ways. First, they can look up past sales records and assist with correct valuations. Second, they can provide valuable information on the current pace (buyer's or sellers') market. Third, they can also negotiate on behalf of the church for the best price. Finally, they are skilled at drafting the Commercial Lease or Purchase Agreement on behalf of the church.

2. **Self-Help Method**:

   Here, you are doing the legwork yourself. It does have some benefits but not many in my opinion. This method controls the pace since you control it directly. If the church is considering buying, it may start by seeking the availability of property adjacent (next door) to the church and contact the owners directly. This can be accomplished by looking online with the local county property appraiser's office. Print out the property owners' names and addresses and contact them. Other information may be available, such as date and price of last purchase, mortgages, and delinquencies of taxes. Leased properties can be found in local trade magazines and newspapers. Third, you may be able to purchase inexpensive drone photographs or video to help with construction and fundraising.

   With this information, you are ready for your board meeting to discuss the details. You can approach the owner yourself since you have the information or bring in a professional Realtor to help negotiate and close the deal. Either way, remember the Lord knows your needs, and He will assist you in ways man cannot. Not all nonprofits start with purchasing land or existing buildings. Most begin by securing a lease or a commercial space.

   I suggest you seek professional help from a realtor to determine the feasibility of purchasing or leasing real estate for your church. Then this professional can assist with either purchasing land/building or lease a commercial space and guide the church through the process.

   If your church is not ready to purchase property yet, leasing is a great option.

Commercial Leases

Maybe holding church at home is becoming impractical and limits your change for growth? Most "church planters" first experience in business and law is the negotiation and execution of a commercial lease. This is often due to the cost. The amount of money needed to rent is much less than purchasing. It is a baby step in commitment. After a lease ends, the church can simply move out and go to another location.

Assuming you have decided upon a place, your next step is entering into a lease agreement with the owner. Although the landlord-tenant law is state specific, allow me to discuss in general terms what a lease is, along with its common components and suggestions for negotiation.

A commercial lease is basically an agreement between the owner of the property and the tenant (church) looking to use the property. Space to hold church is an important part of any ministry. Negotiating a favorable lease puts your church in a better position to grow and succeed.

Remember that a commercial real estate lease agreement is usually drafted and prepared by the landlord's attorney to favor the landlord, not the tenant. Your responsibility as a potential tenant is to read it completely, understand what it says, and then ask for modifications or concessions that will favor your church and strike or negotiate the items you cannot agree to. Knowing what you can afford is the first step.

Determine Your Lease Budget

Probably the most overlooked item is determining your budget. For some reason, I find churches often do not determine how much they can afford for a lease. In other words, clearly understanding all costs contained within a lease agreement. I suggest the church leader be conservative. Also, add in the budget cost items which are the tenant's responsibility such as utilities, maintenance, insurance, and the like. Now that you have established the estimated rent, you can afford to look for comparable spaces.

Research Comparable Rents

The cost of rent is critical to a commercial lease agreement. Do your homework and know what the going costs are in your area so you can negotiate a fair price. Most commercial leases are based on square footage. I suggest considering rent per square foot as well as intangibles such as curb appeal of the property, other tenants in the building, and proper maintenance of the property. Ask yourself, as a congregant, how would I feel parking and entering this building? Would I feel welcome and safe?

Secure a Sample Copy of the Lease

Once you've located a commercial rental location, the landlord may have you complete a rental application. Usually, larger brokers working with the owner will require one. Always request a copy of the proposed lease or sample document. The owner may not give you one but try. This will give you a heads-up on the expected terms and conditions of your lease. You want to review this document before you negotiate terms. Either way, you will be faced with a type of lease common to your area.

Common Types of Commercial Leases

Straight or Gross Lease

This is the most common lease. A fixed amount of monthly rent with no additional charges associated with common ownership expenses. The owner collects the rent and is responsible for the maintenance, insurance, and taxes on the building. Some of these leases may include a minimum cost of repairs; otherwise, the owner pays for them. Also, the owner pays the property taxes for the rented facilities and seeks no reimbursement from the tenant. Finally, the tenant does not share in the insurance costs for the rented building.

Net Leases

A net lease requires the tenant to share responsibility for building expenses with the owner. This type of lease once relegated to strip malls is now seeing common usage in the church world. Sharing in such expenses can be expensive, so reading the fine print is important.

Triple Net (NNN) Leases

This type of lease has the most *expenses* associated with leasing property. It requires the tenant to share all the operating costs of the building the church is renting. This may include the property taxes associated with the building, the insurance costs, and the maintenance. This lease can dramatically increase the overall rental costs.

Percentage Lease

This type of lease requires not only a specified amount of monthly rent but requires the tenant to share with the owner the income derived from the lease. In other words, the landlord charges fixed rent plus collects a percentage of gross sales. This should not apply to a church.

Practice Pointer

Before entering into a lease seek legal counsel to guide you during the process. An experienced attorney can help negotiate the terms and costs in a lease.

Negotiating the Lease

Obligation to Maintain Property:

Usually, the obligation to maintain the property is with the owner or lessor. The owner is responsible for property taxes and insurance. Yet landlords have often required the tenant to share in a pro rata method with these expenses. However, not all landlords do this, so do your due diligence and make sure you negotiate the best deal for the space. Watch out for expenses besides the monthly rental amount.

What type of lease is the landlord asking the church to sign?

It may be a "gross lease," in which all costs are included, or a "net lease" in which there are costs in addition to your rent. Many commercial leases make the tenant responsible for costs such as maintenance or upkeep of common areas. Get the details on these costs up front and negotiate this section to be as favorable as possible. Find out if your church will be responsible for specific systems maintenance and learn the current conditions of those systems so you can estimate costs such as HVAC, electrical, plumbing, etc. Negotiate dollar amount caps to these costs or negotiate for a slightly higher rent in exchange for the landlord taking on all costs. Determine whether there are separate utility meters or if utilities are apportioned among tenants by square footage.

Common items making up a commercial lease.

Rent Amount

Demand the owner or agent to accept what you can afford. Of course, market conditions will control here but as my dad always said: "Nothing ventured, nothing gained." Attempt to secure a gross or straight lease arrangement. This way you avoid the additional expenses mentioned earlier.

Lease Term

Most lease terms last between one and three years. The landlord owner may want to commit you to a longer period. Your budget will determine your commitment. Make sure you feel comfortable before agreeing to any obligations.

Options to Renew:

Flexibility is key. If the owner proposes a longer commitment than you're prepared to accept, consider negotiating an "option to renew." Many church leaders like the idea of a two-year lease including options to continue the lease for another year or two at their discretion. This way, they are not obligated to continue renting when they may not want to stay but have the flexibility to continue with the lease should the rental arrangement work out.

Part of negotiating renewal options includes specifying rent increases. Your landlord may want to increase the rent for each additional year. Consider proposing a limit on rent increases so your lease remains affordable.

Security Deposit

You can also negotiate the amount of your security deposit and the conditions for its return. Keep in mind, in some states, the security deposit within a commercial lease can be used as unpaid rent in case of a breach of contract. Also, beware, some states have no provision for a return of a security deposit in a commercial lease.

Permitted Usage

This lease paragraph describes the conditions under which a tenant agrees to operate the leased space. This limitation may be necessary for insurance reasons, property tax, zoning requirements, or a conflict with an existing tenant. Either way, "light commercial," "medium commercial," "religious use," or "church" are common terms seen in these leases. Again, your local legal counsel will guide you in this area.

Current Condition of Premises

Is the condition of premises in good "swept condition" or fair? You need to access this and include it in the lease. The tenant is usually not responsible for normal wear and tear. Anything beyond that will be charged against the tenants' security deposit. Sometimes the landlord requires the premises to be returned at the end of the lease in "swept clean condition." Some landlords have higher expectations.

Tenant Improvements

You may need to modify the premises to operate as a church. Modifications often include adding walls, bathrooms, and large meeting spaces. Thinking of moving a wall? Building a platform? Try to secure a concession from the landlord to cover that cost to do these renovations. Leverage is most in your favor when considering the space and least in your favor after signing the lease. The landlord may not pay for the renovations but will contribute to close the deal. They may respond to your improvements by requesting a longer lease term. As always, it is up for negotiation. Strike the best deal for you.

Sublease/Assignment

Subleasing is when the tenant leases part or all of their leased space to a third party. Many leases only allow this practice with the landlord's written approval.

Utilities

There are leases where the rent amount includes the utilities. This is becoming less common as the costs of utilities increase. As such, the landlord will require the tenant to have a separate electric meter or share in a pro rata portion of a larger bill. Either way, the tenant typically covers the utility costs. When it comes to garbage, I have seen it sometimes included in the gross rent.

Liability Insurance Requirements

In commercial leases, tenants are commonly required to acquire general liability and premises liability insurance to cover, for example, slip and fall accidents on the premises. This may also include coverage for inventory and equipment in the tenant's space that is lost due to theft or other natural causes. Oftentimes, this requires the tenant to add the landlord as an "additional insured" on the policy. Secure the legal name of the Landlord to inform the insurance carrier. Finally, when it is time for renewal, there may be a requirement to send the landlord a declaration sheet evidencing the renewal of the policy. Failure to renew or the loss of coverage for nonpayment may result in the landlord being notified and then buying the insurance at a higher premium then invoicing the church tenant.

Repairs and Maintenance:

This can become a major liability for the church tenant. Some commercial leases require the tenant to repair HVAC, plumbing and electrical, I have also seen the tenant being responsible for roof repairs. There is generally no reason to accept all this liability. In fact, one can argue some of these repairs are actually capital improvements. Negotiating in this area is critical.

Practice Pointer

Consider agreeing to the first $100- $500 of repairs and the landlord agreeing to cover the remainder. The landlord may consider this since it will prevent minor requests (under $100.00) for repairs. I have seen churches enter a lease with broad repair obligations only to find a major repair not long after signing the lease. Finally, negotiate a cap, annual or otherwise, on any repairs.

Designated Parking

Knowing where your staff, congregants, and visitors can park is critical. Although important to the church it is sometimes not discussed or addressed in the commercial lease. This is especially important if the church leases a space in a strip mall or urban area. Parking spaces come at a premium, and if there are other tenants, complications can arise should your congregant park in an area used by other commercial tenants for their customers. Your tenant neighbors pay rent too. Avoid conflict. Have the lease highlight the area(s) where and when those visiting or working staff can park.

Practice Pointer

Include in your lease an "exhibit page" outlining the property along with highlighting the parking area your staff, visitors, and congregants may park. Also note the times of days those spaces can be used. Such clear indications avoid conflict and by incorporating an exhibit to the lease. The exhibit becomes incorporated into the lease and is binding on the parties, however, this must be done before signing or executing the lease; otherwise, the Landlord may not approve it later.

Signage

Having adequate signage is important for any business, including churches. Whether it is advertising to the public or giving directional signs in the building landlords restrict signage due to limited space, conflicts with fellow tenants, or fear of damaging the building. As such, the church lease needs to address this. Most leases use simple language stating signage requires the approval of the landlord. This is unacceptable for a church. Like parking, this issue should be addressed prior to signing the lease.

Practice Pointer

Signage also needs to be settled upfront and included as an exhibit. Have a diagram of the building along with the specific leased space and designate on the diagram the signage the church desires to use. Be specific. You want to include the measurements of the signage, colors, and even a likeness of the signs. Include all the signs you wish to place both in the interior and exterior of the building(s). Will an electric sign have certain needs? Have this issue agreed to and signed off by the landlord prior to signing the lease. It is usually easier to negotiate this before you execute the lease. Then the exhibit needs to be included and incorporated as part of the lease.

Default and Remedy Clauses

Read the terms of your commercial property lease as it pertains to default and/or termination of the lease. You'll want a clause that allows you time to cure a default before eviction. I always consider including a "liquidation clause." This clause limits the liability in case of default to a set amount of monetary damages. The amount agreed can be one- or two-month's rent instead of the entire amount remaining on the lease. You also will want to negotiate any penalties for early termination of the lease should you decide you need to leave before the lease term is up. As a final note, be aware of "automatic renewal triggers." Such provisions provide that the lease will be renewed for another term should you fail to notify the landlord in writing, within so many days, prior to vacating the premises at the end of term.

In summary, when it comes to commercial leases, be proactive and negotiate changes to the lease ahead of time. Seriously consider these strategies and options. Think of more scenarios particular to your church's needs. As the saying goes, "fortune favors the brave." Of course, I strongly urge you to retain competent legal counsel to represent your interests.

What if you are already in a lease and have been saving money to purchase property and you're ready to move towards purchasing? If this is the case, the remainder of this chapter will discuss the issues involved in purchasing real property. We will discuss authorization to purchase, drafting the contract to purchase with its provisions, and the process through closing. Let's get started.

Purchasing Real Estate

A common method to help your church grow or maintain its growth is to purchase property for building or expansion. It allows the physical footprint to accommodate the additional congregants. On the other hand, even if your church is not growing at this time, you may want to buy property for future planning efforts. Additional property purchases allow what I call the "flexibility factor" to assist in attaining more space if needed later or to fulfill master plans for growth. Worst case scenario, you can always sell it later to fund current ministry projects. So where should you start? After praying, start determining your budget.

Determining Your Purchase Budget

Like most major purchases, church leaders must determine how much a church can spend or carry in case of a loan on purchasing real estate. What can the church budget handle on a cash purchase or making mortgage payments? How much are the monthly gross payments? Each mortgage payment commonly has four main components: principal, interest, taxes, and insurance. You will most likely be able to remove property taxes from the total amount since a successful application for ad valorem exemption would remove such a financial burden on the church. But principal, interest, and insurance are a mainstay.

What resources are available for a deposit to secure the property? Is there readily available money to write the check to the sellers' attorney or title company to bind the property by contract? This must be addressed. In many states, any real estate contract must have a deposit of money or "consideration" tied to the contract to make the contract valid and enforceable.

Preliminary Authorization to Proceed

After determining your budget and before making the purchase, it is important to secure and document approval of the governing body. This can be the membership or board of directors or both. I suggest you accomplish this by addressing four issues. First, approval to proceed with investigating property purchase. Second, securing the services of a real estate professional to assist with the process. Third, retaining the services of a real estate attorney. Fourth, approval to proceed with funding sources.

Approval to proceed with investigating the property purchase - Who has authority to authorize the purchase?

Churches, being nonprofit corporations, typically require either denominational authority approval, board of directors and/or membership approval, or a combination for property purchases. Check your governing documents such as the articles of incorporation (charter), constitution, and/or bylaws for the authority to bind the corporation to a purchase. Keep in mind, the underwriter for the title policy will most likely require a resolution approving the purchase from such authority, so taking care of this early in the process will prevent a later headache.

Secure a Realtor: Key to Negotiations

The church realtor has access to information the church may not have and can demand things you may not feel comfortable requesting. Yes, this is important. Your local real estate attorney has their role, but it is typically separate and different from the real estate agent. The realtor can assist with negotiations, scheduling inspections, and other like items requiring "boots on the ground." As an attorney, I do not feel threatened by a realtor but see them as part of the team helping my client get across the goal line on the transaction. Remember, the seller pays the real estate commission, not the church as a buyer. Those who say the Buyer gets the property cheaper if they do not retain a realtor are usually wrong. The sales price is according to the market, not whether the buyer has a realtor or not.

Retain the Services of a Professional–Hiring Legal Counsel

This is important especially at the earliest part of the process. Your own legal counsel will advise you according to local requirements such as approved or designated zoning, sufficiency of seller's title, liens, encumbrances, environmental matters, and the like. Your attorney will also be interested in other issues such as, but not limited to, whether your offer should contain any contingencies. (More on contingencies later in this chapter).

Approval to Proceed with Contract Purchase

Obtaining authorization to proceed is important. Once the governing authority of the church should approve these legal actions the next step is to retain competent professionals to write up the contract and assist with securing a mortgage, if necessary.

Basic Elements of a Contract to Purchase

Each contract has its own terms guided by its state laws. Although each state may vary in its requirements, there are certain common elements as follows:

1. Name the buyer making the offer, along with their corporate designation if necessary.
2. Name of the seller of the property in question, along with their corporate designation if necessary.
3. Street address of the property in question.
4. Legal description of the property in question.
5. Price for the property and amounts of deposit(s), including deadlines to bind the contract.
6. The name and address of the escrow agent to receive the deposit(s), Closing Agent to perform the closing, and issue the title insurance policy.
7. Description of the transaction: cash or contingent on financing? If financing is involved, what are the terms, rate, and other details.
8. The closing dates.
9. Survey option by the buyer.
10. Title commitment and who is paying for it.
11. Timeframe to cure any title defects.
12. Inspection period and timeframe for buyer to cancel contract.
13. Parties' addresses for notices to be made under agreement.
14. Warranties, representations, and disclosures of seller.

15. Warranties and representations of purchaser.

16. Miscellaneous provisions.

17. Effective date and signature of parties

Although there will be other provisions, the outlined items above represent the most common.

Essentials for a Purchase Agreement

Offer, acceptance and consideration are necessary for a purchase agreement. Most people do not realize that once you make an *offer,* and it is *accepted* by the other party, you may have a binding contract. So, making an offer on a piece of property is serious business. What makes an offer binding? Generally speaking, when an offer in writing is made with *consideration* and then it is accepted by all parties.

"Consideration" is defined in Black's Law Dictionary (8th Edition) as "something bargained for and received by a promisor from a promisee: that which motivates a person to do something, especially to engage in a legal act."[18] Black's continues to state, "Consideration is necessary for an agreement to be enforceable."[19] Thus, it is important to make a deposit or agree to make a deposit within a few days of the offer to make the contract binding. Local law will guide you here.

Other contracts may not require deposits or consideration to be enforceable. But as a general rule, real estate requires it. What makes a written and executed contract necessary? Why can't it be an oral contract like shaking of hands? Well, here we have to discuss a legal term called "statute of frauds."

The "Statute of frauds" is defined in Black's Legal Dictionary (8th Edition) as "A 1677 English Statute that declared certain contracts judicially unenforceable (but not void) if they were not committed to writing and signed by the party to be charged."[20] This has traditionally applied to real estate contracts. State law may vary.

So let us sum it up. A valid written *offer* for a piece of real estate is presented with a money deposit (consideration) to the owner of the property which becomes a *contract* upon the seller's written acceptance. Only make an offer when you are ready to be bound in a contract. Do not make multiple offers to different sellers

18 Garner, Black's Law Dictionary, 8th Edition, Page 324

19 Garner, Black's Law Dictionary, 8th Edition, Page 324

20 Garner, Black's Law Dictionary, 8th Edition, Page 1450

since you may be bound to each one. Local legal counsel will guide you on the law in your state.

For an effective contract it is necessary to include with your offer not only a deposit but a deadline for your offer to be accepted. Most contracts also include a requirement to state the closing date. You want to make sure the closing is scheduled far enough in advance so you can make your preparations to buy the property. More on the closing later.

Besides the price or consideration paid, the contract should have a complete description of the property involved in the transaction. Most common is a street address, legal description, and finally a "folio" or property ID number used by the local county property appraiser's office.

Before the contract is executed and enforceable, I wish to point out several items of interest. They are contract contingencies sometimes included in the contract.

Contract Contingencies–Contingent Offers.

Sometimes the buyer is not ready, willing, or able to close unless a certain future event takes place first. When an offer is designed this way, it is a contract subject to a secondary event or contingency. For example, the contract is contingent on the sale of the buyer's property first.

Blacks Law Dictionary 8th edition defines a contingency as is "An event that may or may not occur; a possibility."[21] Here, I will highlight several common contingencies which may or may not apply to your transaction. Your attorney may think of more due to your local laws.

Risk with Contingencies

Presenting an offer with contingencies is risky since the seller may be reluctant to accept the buyer's offer. There are some legitimate reasons for the seller's hesitancy. First, by accepting an offer with a contingency, the property will be off the market until the contingency is satisfied. Second, the seller may also miss other offers which do not contain such contingencies. Third, during the contingency period the seller will have to continue maintaining and paying property expenses and taxes while the buyers' contingencies are fulfilled.

21 Garner, Black's Law Dictionary, 8nd Edition, Page 338

Practice Pointer

If you need to make an offer with contingencies, draft in some language enticing the seller to consider it. The buyer can offer to reimburse the seller at closing for certain expenses caused by the delay. The seller may be attracted to your offer knowing the delayed property taxes or maintenance costs accrued during the contingency period will be reimbursed by the buyer. Another suggestion is for the buyer to offer the seller a credit for a certain sum of money (i.e., $5,000) at closing for going through the waiting period.

Contingencies are Important

Placing contingencies in contracts is important. First, because the buyer may need to clear certain hurdles before committing to the agreement. This may be because the financing may be necessary in order to close the deal. Second, although the buyer may be ready to close the transaction, the property itself may not be acceptable. This may be because of current zoning not being compatible with the intended use. Third, the buyer may need to verify the areas of property via a survey to make sure the property fits for the ministry's purposes.

Contingencies Have Risks

Whatever the reason, contingent offers have risks. There are several reasons for this. First, the seller may be reluctant to accept your offer because by accepting, the property will be off the market until the contingencies are cleared or satisfied. Second, the market may turn against the seller while the contingencies are being satisfied. Third, a contract without contingencies will more likely proceed to closing without any hiccups or delays. Fourth, the longer it takes to fulfill the contingencies the more likely there could be an interest rate change. More on that later. Finally, an offer without contingencies allows the buyer to negotiate from a stronger position.

Now that we know contingencies have risks and benefits let us look at the most common contingencies contained in real estate contracts.

Examples of Contingencies

Contract Contingent on Inspection and Approval by Buyer

Although common in residential contracts, this contingency occasionally surfaces in commercial agreements. Basically, this contingency allows the buyer to back out of the contract prior to the end of the inspection period if the inspection discovers something which the Buyer does not like. Usually, the language is broad, allowing the buyer to get out of the contract and have the deposit returned. This contingency also requires the buyer to notify the seller in writing if the buyer decides to exercise its right to terminate the contract. In turn, the closing agent is required to refund the deposit back to the buyer, thus ending the transaction. This contingency is a great weapon in the buyer's arsenal should the buyer want out.

Contract Contingent on Appraisal

Another contingency is an appraisal contingency. Here, the contract is contingent upon the buyer obtaining, usually at their own expense, a satisfactory written appraisal from a licensed appraiser. The appraisal provides an independent value of the property based on prior sales. For the contract to proceed the appraised value usually must meet or exceed the contract price. If the purchase is being financed the lender will require this. The buyer may choose to notify the seller of the appraisal amount and either terminate the contract—in which case the deposit will be returned, thereby releasing the buyer and seller from all further obligations under the contract— *or* change the purchase price to match the appraisal. The parties may agree to remove this contingency and continue with the contract "as is" unless the buyer's lender requires the appraisal. They usually do. Getting an appraisal waived by the lender is unlikely. Usually if the appraised amount comes in less than the purchase price, the lender may require the buyer to come to closing with more money.

Contract Contingent on Buyer Securing Financing

If the buyer agrees to pay cash at closing, then the contract moves quicker through the process because financing is then not necessary and there are no lender documents or requirements. But what if the buyer does not have the cash to buy the property outright? Here, we will address financing the purchase by the buyer.

When it comes to financing, the buyer has two options when writing the contingency. First, purchase a money note and mortgage. Second, third-party financing.

When choosing the purchase money option, the buyer asks for the seller to finance the deal or "hold paper." Should the buyer decide to notify the seller that the purchase will be funded by a purchase money note and mortgage, certain facts must be declared in the contract, such as the interest rate of the note and the terms or length of the note. For example, a 30 year note with a fixed interest rate of 7%. The parties can negotiate the particulars. With a purchase money note and mortgage, the buyer and seller agree to the terms. But should the buyer wish to have third party financing go to a commercial bank, denominational lender, or other third party, such terms and conditions are much less flexible.

Either way, it is critical to declare such required terms to protect the buyer and inform the seller of the acceptable terms. For example, the buyer should declare the maximum rate it will pay on the note. This is advisable since the interest rate markets for mortgages are in a constant flux. One day, the rate is favorable and the next week may not. But have no fear, many commercial lenders or third-party lenders would be happy to "lock" your rate for a fee! The more contingencies the buyer has, the longer the rate lock should be.

Final comment: usually the contract will require the buyer, using third-party financing, to use good faith and be diligent to obtain loan approval or face default under the contract and lose the deposit.

Contract Contingent on Property being Rezoned for Religious Usage

Verify the property can be used for the purpose you intend. If it is an adjacent or bordering parcel, your local authorities may look favorably on rezoning, but this is no guarantee. Many churches are facing more and more hostile local governing agencies due to the loss of property tax revenue.

You may state in the contract that closing is contingent on rezoning to protect the church. I have noticed the following language used. *"This contract is contingent upon the buyer receiving all governmental and zoning approvals, waiting periods, and receipt of all permits for use of the property to build a church or school. Sellers will cooperate with this process and provide whatever material or signatures are required."* Keep in mind, it is imperative to receive the proper language from your own local legal counsel.

Contract Contingent on an Acceptable Survey

A contract contingent on an approved survey is important. Basically, it is a clause requiring a third-party surveyor to complete a survey of the property before the sale is finalized. It is important to know what one is buying, and a survey reveals just that! The language in this clause states the survey must meet certain criteria, such as confirming the boundaries of the property and identifying any encroachments. This contingency may also provide language allowing the buyer to walk away from the sale if the survey results are not satisfactory.

Contract Contingent on Simultaneous Closing

Here, the contract is contingent on simultaneous closing of another property owned by the Seller or Buyer. This is an agreement between two parties that allows each party to close on their respective properties at the same time. Both parties agree to wait until both transactions are completed before any money can change hands and close. This contingency is common in residential real estate transactions but not necessarily common in commercial transactions.

Contract Contingent on Buyer's Attorney Approval

This contingency is often used to protect the buyer who desires to retain legal counsel for the transaction. The contingency contained within the contract makes the transaction contingent on the buyer's attorney's review and approval of the agreement. The process is rather straightforward. The buyer will have his or her attorney review the contract and advise the buyer on the legal implications of the agreement and then suggest proceeding or not. Once the buyer's attorney has approved the agreement, the buyer will have the option to proceed.

Practice Pointer

A final thought before we move on. It may be tempting to waive contingencies or not include them to make your offer more competitive. Keep in mind, including contingencies are important to protect you. When making an offer, it is important to strike a balance between acceptable contingencies to protect the buyer (church) while presenting a competitive offer to the Seller.

Survey

Importance of a Survey of the Real Property

What is a survey? Technically, it is a document that determines the boundaries or footprint of the subject property. It will show what the church is buying and the adjacent property abutting it. Knowing your boundary is important so you can visualize in your mind the available space to build a church building or to see if the property fits in your master plan. Also, the dimensions of existing building(s) on the property.

After you have reviewed the document, it is helpful to ask the surveyor to go over it with you. But be aware, he or she may not remember the property in much detail. Always walk around the property before closing. You will notice the surveyor's pink flags or stakes designating the boundaries of the subject property. Take pictures because usually those flags will be removed by either weather or a kid looking to have fun with them.

This will not only give you a feel for the size of the parcel and the landscape but also any noticeable deficiencies to raise with the seller before closing.

Additionally, the survey will also help you determine whether there is adequate space, not only for the building but also for parking. Here, an architect can assist you. Most municipalities have guidelines for how many parking spaces a certain property size can accommodate. This will also be guided by the size of the building's square footage. Regardless of such details, a qualified architect can help you. The architect not only knows the local laws and regulations for parking space requirements, but also the required number of handicap spots.

To secure a survey, contact your real estate agent or attorney. The cost is usually reasonable for the information you receive. But on balance, it is extremely valuable. The survey will reveal to the buyer exactly what they are purchasing. Plus, it will delineate any encroachments or easements on the property. What are they?

Encroachments

Encroachments are defined in Black's Law Dictionary 8th Edition as "an interference with or intrusion onto another's property."[22] Exactly how much any encroachment will interfere with your use will be the focus of your attention.

A common encroachment is when a neighbor's fence crosses onto your property. At times, a party will put up a fence and not give the fence company a current survey to go by. A more serious encroachment is when a neighbor's building or driveway lies or encroaches on the subject property.

22 Black, Black's Law Dictionary, 8th Edition, Page 568

Easements

An easement is a little more technical. Easements are defined in Black's Law Dictionary 8th Edition as "an interest in land owned by another person, consisting in the right to use or control the land, or an area above or below it, for a specific limited purpose such as to cross it for access to a public road." [23] It is a burden on the land which does not yield any benefit to you. For example, it may also allow access to an electrical or cable line.

The title commitment will state any county, city, and municipal easements for roads, utilities, and other purposes. This way the buyer knows about them. For encroachments, the survey will guide you. Easements are common. Encroachments are less common. Your local legal counsel can assist guiding the church about them.

Purchase Title Insurance or Attorney Title

Most contracts for purchase of real property require that an updated abstract (a chronologically arranged compilation of all recorded documents affecting title to a property) or attorney/title insurance be provided. Attorney title/title insurance is a contract whereby the insurer (insurance company) agrees to protect the insured (church) against property value loss through a defect in the title. The title defect is an irregularity or issue in the chain of title. Examples can be liens, judgments, forged documents, and errors in the public records.

Verify the title insurance is being issued under the church's correct legal name. Additionally, make sure the property description is complete with the monetary coverage equaling at least the gross purchase price.

Determining the insurance requirements (hazard, flood etc.) is important. If required or desired, secure insurance binders for the closing agent.

What about the lender? Will they be protected against title issues post-closing? Yes, they will. If property is being purchased with financing, the lender will require a title insurance policy. The fee for the bank's policy is usually paid for by the borrower.

23 Black, Black's Law Dictionary, 8th Edition Page 548

Practice Pointer

The church should consider buying its own title insurance policy if it is purchasing real estate. If financing is involved the church will be paying for the lender's title policy. But keep in mind this policy only protects the lender not the church. Paying extra for the owner's title policy adds an additional measure of protection to the investment against title issues which may come up in the future. Final thought -make sure the amount of title insurance equals the full purchase price of the property. Lenders title policy will be less since it covers the amount of the mortgage which is usually less than the purchase price.

Closing

Closing Date

When drafting the purchase agreement, it is important to include a "closing date." Leave enough days from the execution or signing date to the closing to allow time for the survey, financing, contingencies, and other terms to be completed.

Practice Pointer

A tight closing date may result in a failed closing or an addendum request to the seller to extend the closing. This places the buyer's deposit at risk. Keep in mind the contract may have a provision stating, "time is of the essence." Much angst and stress can result from a tight closing date. I always suggest extra time to close just to make sure you have time to appropriately complete your due diligence. Parties can mutually agree to move up the closing date if both parties are ready to close.

Closing Documents

Before closing, the closing agent needs to send you the closing package, which contains the papers you will have to sign at closing. Although ALL documents are important there are three deserving of special attention to review prior to closing: the note/mortgage, deed, and settlement statement.

If the property is being financed, it is important to review carefully the note/mortgage. The note is a written promise to pay another a certain sum of money at a certain time. Basically, it evidences your indebtedness. In some states, the mortgage and note are a combined document. In some jurisdictions, they are separate. Focus on the note. Verify the interest rate and term (length of the mortgage) are correct. Make sure the note matches your lock in amount or rate guarantee when you applied. If it does not, ask the lender, why?

Be on the lookout for any "guarantor" provisions in the note. These provisions require those who sign personally guarantee the payoff of the mortgage. A church loan should not contain personal guarantees from the officers and/or directors. Additionally, when signing the note, any church officer or director should verify they are signing in their corporate capacity (e.g., John Jones, as President). This evidences your signature as a corporate agent and not as an individual. Finally, beware of signing multiple notes. There is no reason to run the risk of owing more than the purchase price. The one exception is a HECM (Home Equity Conversion Mortgage) loan from HUD but a church would not apply for this type of loan.

Transactions with a loan will typically have two sets of closing documents: title company documents and the "loan package." Together they make up the "closing package." Do not be surprised if one package is ready and the closing agent is waiting on the other. In my experience, it is usually the lender package which holds things up.

Warranty Deed

A deed transfers legal ownership of the property. The warranty deed provides the church with a warranty of title providing a bundle of rights, unavailable through a "quit claim" deed. The Quit Claim deed only transfers what ownership the Grantor has which may or may not be as comprehensive in rights which a Warranty Deed includes. The warranty deed provides the grantee or person receiving the property comprehensive land ownership. All title policies I have seen require the church to receive a warranty deed.

Practice Pointer

The deed should be reviewed closely. First, make sure the marital status of the seller(s) or grantor(s) is stated correctly. If the seller is married, ask that the spouse also sign the deed. If the seller or grantor is divorced, verify such by asking the closing agent to secure the "final judgment" papers showing the property was in fact conveyed to the seller. Second, the legal description on the deed must be identical to the deed he/she received and as set forth in the title insurance commitment or attorney title. Third, the deed will state "exceptions" or items excluded in the transfer of a free title. Generally common exceptions in the deed are taxes for the current year, easements, restrictions, covenants of record, zoning ordinances, etc. Fourth, the deed must be signed using the full and complete names of all the grantors as set forth in the title insurance commitment or attorney title. They must be executed with witnesses and notary as required in your state. The church's legal counsel will advise on the deed's sufficiency and title policy.

Settlement Statement

This document itemizes the seller's and buyer's expenses and discloses the settlement charges for such items as prorated taxes, title search, recording fees, city/county tax/stamps, state tax/stamps, survey, etc. Review the statement carefully and make sure the other party (seller) is paying for the items the Seller is responsible for according to the contract. Watch for unnecessary charges being included because of an oversight. My experience with many closing agents is they are very diligent in what they do. Please be kind to them since they work on many files with deadlines. Subject to your attorney's review and approval, you may proceed to closing.

Closing the Deal

Make sure you contact the closing agent about time and place. Find out from the closing agent what you need to bring and who needs to attend the closing. Always bring identification with you. Oftentimes, certain documents require notarization. Rest assured, as you sit at the table, the closing agent will explain every document to you prior to signing. Having your legal counsel present will also give added assurance. Relax, you have done your homework, and your attorney was there from the beginning. Let it be an enjoyable experience.

When done, ask the closing agent to provide a hard copy or to e-mail copies of the closing package which will contain all of the executed documents. Ask when you can expect the church owners title policy to be mailed or emailed for your permanent records.

Conclusion

We have discussed real estate in general and commercial leases and property purchases specifically for your church. Whether to lease or purchase is a question unique to the church. Some feel more comfortable securing a leased space while others choose to purchase. Some choose to secure the services of professionals to assist while others feel they can take care of this matter themselves. Regardless of the choice, the church must have the financial resources available to move forward. Unfortunately, most churches do not have money readily available. As such, they require financing to move into a leased space or to purchase. The next chapter discusses a church's options when securing financing.

Action Points for the Next 30 Days:

1. Create a budget to ensure the lease or purchase is financially feasible and will not place the church in financial jeopardy
2. Before proceeding to purchase or lease property, has the leadership secured proper written board and/or membership authorization to proceed?
3. Has the church retained the proper professionals to help guide the church through the process? (e.g., realtor, attorney)
4. Prior to closing, ask the closing agent to send you key documents ahead of time for a no-rush review (e.g., mortgage, note, deed, title policy)

CHAPTER

10

Church Lending Options

A pastor called my office about a line of credit transaction the church was considering. The minister sheepishly said early in the application process the board signed a document stating the church congregation had met and voted, approving the line of credit although the members never voted. I asked him why they did that? He said at the time, the board felt the church governing documents did not require it and voted to sign it anyway, believing it was necessary to proceed with the loan application. But later, they realized they created a larger problem. The lender was now proceeding with the transaction under a false impression the church membership approved the loan. The pastor did not know what to do now except to say, "We should have retained you. I know you would have advised us then against doing this, and we could have avoided this whole problem." Well, that is true.

Important Comment: Financing and lending is local. This Chapters discussion and examples may very well be different from the reader's experience. This should be expected.

Investigate Available Funding Sources

Unlike many years ago, there are several funding **sources and processes** for churches to choose from. In this chapter, we will discuss the available funding sources and their advantages and disadvantages. Then we will discuss creating a financing packet to assist the church in securing the funding. Let us begin with the simple and common funding source: the line of credit.

Line of Credit

The simplest way to seek funding, whether to purchase property or to meet operating expenses, is by applying for a line of credit. To qualify for a line of credit it is common to have the line secured by church property. It is usually given to the church by its current checking/lending institution. Once "the line" is established, the church will receive a checkbook to draw on your line, Though, the simplest way to draw is by electronically transferring money from the line to the church operating account.

A line of credit is different from a fixed mortgage instrument. The line is usually set up with a five year duration note. In other words, after five years, the note balance must be paid in full. The exception is if the lender grants a renewal/extension of the line or offers converting the line to permanent financing. Often, the interest rate is above the current prime rate or the rate given to the strongest bank customers. It is also common to have a note tied to a floating loan rate for this type of financing. This means the interest rate will change according to current market conditions at a certain point in time.

How do you receive a line of credit? I suggest you contact the bank where your church's checking or operating account is situated. Set an appointment with a commercial loan account representative and request an application for a line of credit. They are standard in the industry.

A line of credit has certain benefits. First, it is inexpensive. Often the closing costs are nominally paid for by the lender. Second, this loan offers immediate access to cash should a need arise. For example, immediate cash may be needed in case of a disaster, an opportunity to make a deposit to buy property, or to meet unexpected operating expenses. The drawbacks are associated closing costs should the bank not pay for them. Outside of that, it is a flexible lending option for your church.

Denominational Financing

An often overlooked method of financing is the opportunities one has with their affiliated fellowships or denomination. Several denominations offer financing options for small and large churches. Do you know the opportunities available through your denomination or fellowship? Do not overlook these opportunities for available financing. If one is not available to you then consider the next conventional financing.

Conventional or Bank Financing

This loan method is the most common. With a conventional loan, the church borrows a sum of money from the bank or other lending institutions and promises to repay the borrowed amount (principal) over a period of time (term), plus a charge for the use of the money (interest). For many years, a local bank would not consider a loan to a church. The understated reason was foreclosure. Most local banks do not want to risk the bad publicity to foreclose and sell a church facility. But times have changed. Now banks and credit unions are common funding sources for churches.

The question is does the institution where your church does its banking offer loans to churches? If it does, this may be the best starting place to secure a loan. There are several reasons for this. First, they know the church and already have a record of its deposits and withdrawals (i.e., capacity to service a loan). Second, the church may already have a relationship with the lender and may even know some loan officers already. Finally, there is the matter of convenience which is a big benefit.

However, the banks that do loan money to churches generally do so without permanent financing. In other words, do not expect a 30 year mortgage. The church loan is usually for five to seven years in duration and then the interest rate is renegotiated or the loan is called in for payment. What is typical? With conventional bank loans, the church loan will be amortized for a period of time, say 30 or 15 years, but it will probably contain a "balloon" feature. A balloon is a note or promise to pay, which becomes due at a certain point in time. A five to ten year balloon is common.

For example, a loan amortized for thirty years with a seven year balloon comes due in full at the end of year seven for the outstanding loan balance minus the principal paid during the seven years.

Is it possible to renew a note? Yes, many banks will renew the loan with additional costs, but understand, they may not have too. Should the bank not agree to extend the mortgage, this places the church in the precarious position of either seeking alternative financing or paying off the note. Some banks offer adjustable rate loans that can expose your church to substantially increased loan payments if interest rates rise. Most of these adjustable rate mortgages are tied to the "prime" plus a premium. The prime rate is the interest rate at which banks loan money to their best customers, or it is set according to the "federal funds rate." For example, prime plus 1½ points means, assuming the prime is at six percent (6%), the rate would be seven and one half percent (7.5%).

Practice Pointer

Who knows when the Federal Reserve Bank should choose to raise or lower rates or how high or low they will go? During the 1970s, the prime rate was upwards of 21%. Seeking fixed financing should be seriously considered. This lack of long term fixed rate financing has made bond financing for churches a consideration.

Bond Financing

Bond financing has taken hold in the church financial world although in recent years it has waned, in my opinion, due to the opening of bank conventional financing. What does it mean to have bond financing or to "float" a bond issue? In bond financing, the church, instead of going to a bank for a loan, contacts a bond company who secures the loan proceeds from private and/or institutional investors. The investors exchange their investment proceeds for issuing a loan.

The process is rather straightforward. The church contacts a bond company who specializes in nonprofit corporations such as schools and churches. Keep in mind, bond companies are different from your local bank in that the money comes from individual and/or institutional investors or bond holders. The bonds are usually sold to investors in $1,000 increments. The total size of the bond issuance is equal to the amount of money needed by the church/borrower, plus costs and expenses.

The process is as follows: once approved, the bond company seeks to secure the finances for the church by contacting investors who will invest in the boards to be issued for the church or school thus financing the loan. This type of financing is more costly than the traditional bank loan. Also, when calculating the amount of the loan, it is important to remember, if necessary, to request the bond company to finance or "wrap" these costs (i.e., audit, bond company fees, and attorney fees, etc.) in the loan.

Once the loan is closed and the proceeds are disbursed, the church then makes its principle and interest payments to the bondholders through the corporate trustee. The trustee handles record keeping and payment functions. The church payments are deposited in a special account called a "sinking fund." In this fund, the church's payments are held and are withdrawn when the bond holders' interest or principle payments are necessary. Trustees fees may also be paid from the sinking fund.

In this world of financing, not all bond issues are the same. There may be other types of bond financing, but I have grouped them into two types: "best efforts" and "firm underwriting." Once you understand each type, you can choose which best suits your congregational needs. Let's take a look at them.

A. Best Efforts

This type of issue requires the church to sell the bonds itself, often with the help of the bonding company. In essence, once the bond company and the church agree on the amount of financing and the costs, a bond company representative visits your church and explains the benefits of a bond issue. Then their representative will ask the members to buy the bonds they are selling. This is typically associated with a type of capital fund raising campaign.

Specifically, the bonds can be purchased in two ways. First, the bonding company sells them the bond at face value (usually $1,000 per bond), and the member writes a check for the purchase. Second, the member agrees to buy the bond purchase but makes payments over time. Once the final installment payment is made, the bond is issued to the member. Church members can buy one or more bonds. The amount of bonds sold will equal the necessary amount of financing the church needs for its project plus costs and expenses.

There are positives and negatives to the best efforts method of bond financing.

The *positive(s)* are lower costs for the church versus a firm underwriting campaign, which we will discuss next. Additionally, the church members invest in their own church which can result in a type of "buy in" with the church project.

The *negative(s)* are people sometimes consider bond purchasing as donations, which they are not. They do not give the church money but lend the church money. For it to be a donation, they have to subsequently forgive the indebtedness. As a result of this confusion, it may have a detrimental effect on any subsequent capital contribution campaign to reduce debt or to raise additional money to pay off the bonds.

On balance, best efforts is a type of bond financing which is done in-house with lower costs. But as we discussed, there are positives and negatives to this option.

For those reasons another type of bond issue has emerged, and that is the "firm underwriting" bond issuance.

B. Firm Underwriting

With a firm underwriting issue, no bonds are sold to your congregation, unless it is agreed between the church and the issuer. Generally, with this method, the bond company underwrites your loan by first committing to purchase all of your bonds and selling them to their investors. The church members and attenders do not have to buy any bonds. By agreeing to buy all the bonds, the church is guaranteed to receive the funds needed.

There are a couple *advantage*s to the firm underwriting method:

1. The bond company guarantees all bonds will be sold.
2. There is no confusion about considering bond purchases as "donations" since they are not sold through the congregation.

There are also a couple *disadvantage*s to this method:

1. The costs and expenses associated with this method are generally higher than best efforts.
2. Since bond sales are guaranteed, the fees are higher than the best-efforts method.

Overall, firm underwriting costs more, but the transaction is much smoother. So, for a premium, the church is guaranteed all bonds will be sold and financing will become available after closing. "You get what you pay for."

Bond Financing in General

Bond issuance is a great option for many churches. Unfortunately, Bond issues are becoming scarce for churches, but they are now mostly being used by church schools. Every church must weigh the advantages a bond issue provides to them as compared to traditional lending methods. Whether the church decides in favor of "best efforts" or "firm underwriting," bond financing is a viable alternative. Unlike commercial bank balloon loans, bond issues also have the distinct advantage of offering a long term fixed rate which may not be available through traditional lenders or denominational financing. Bonds are also generally fully amortized over a fifteen to twenty year period, providing a level debt service which aids in budgeting and ensures that the loan can eventually be retired without the hassle of refinancing a balloon loan.

From a planning standpoint, you may want to request the bond company to include a prepayment provision, allowing the church to prepay your bonds, in whole or part, without premium or penalty. If allowed, the prepayment will probably have to come out of the general operating account of the church.

Bond Financing Liability to Board Members

Yes, church board members or directors may face personal liability for issuing bonds if they violate state or federal securities laws. This happens when a church issues unregistered, nonexempt securities or utilizes the services of unlicensed agents. How does the church leadership avoid this? First, resist the "save money and do it ourselves" mentality. Second, it is important to seek the services of a licensed professional securities firm/agent who follows the federal and state laws associated with church bond issues. Third, keep in mind, the church liability insurance policy may not cover the church for securities law violations. As such, the church and/or board members may be on the hook for their own attorney fees and resulting jury or bench verdict. So, tread carefully and proceed only with professional bond company and legal guidance.

Importance of Legal Counsel in Bond or Other Financing Transactions

Keep in mind, financing involves complex negotiations and documents. The issuing of bonds is a complex legal process. As such, retaining the services of competent legal counsel will go a long way in assuring a smooth transaction and avoiding legal problems later. An attorney should be engaged in the earliest part of the process through closing. These documents can have a profound impact on the church if they are not drafted and reviewed carefully. Keep in mind, the lender will have an underwriter and legal counsel looking out for their interests but not necessarily the churches.

Corporate Resolution Authorizing the Loan and Retaining Professionals

Regardless of the method of financing chosen, the church needs to have the governing body of the church approve the loan transaction. This will most likely be its board of directors. Always check your governing documents for such provisions. But keep in mind, some lenders (bond or bank) may have a requirement to secure membership approval for any large loan.

As such, draft a corporate resolution authorizing the loan transaction and the company you will be securing the loan from. This includes particulars of the loan such as amount, lending provisions, and costs in the resolution. I also suggest including authorization to retain a professional(s) to assist in the matter. In the resolution, you may want to include clear authorization designating the agent(s) to sign the legal documents for closing.

Regardless of the method of financing, whether it is denominational, commercial, or a bond issuance, certain steps should be taken before the application process to assure approval and success. First is the "financing packet." Let's look at that next.

Financing Packet

Regardless of the type of loan, before applying, the church needs to gather some information for the lender. This information is critical to assist the lender in approving the loan. This gathering is often called the "financing packet." I suggest preparing this financing packet of information prior to contacting the lender.

Items to Include

This packet will contain various documents to assist your denomination, bank, or bond company in determining your trustworthiness for financing. Remember, creditors are in the business to assess risk. Informing them of your creditworthiness and capacity/financial ability for a loan payment is key. Therefore, providing the lender with a packet of information demonstrating your worthiness and capacity to service a loan assists in its approval.

This is not in any way an exhaustive list, and you may want to supplement it with more information. But since the goal is to get approved, at least consider the following:

Church Biography

You want to present to the lender a brief history of the church, including when and how it started. Consider also providing a detailed description of the senior or lead pastor, especially if he or she has good tenure demonstrating longevity and stability. Continue by providing a statement on the mission and purpose of the entity. Conclude with the impact the church has made on the community and how the loan would be used to further such contributions.

Legal Documents

Write a paragraph stating what governing documents the church has and attach them to the packet as exhibits. Such documents may include:

1. Articles of Incorporation or Charter
2. Constitution
3. Bylaws
4. Board resolution to proceed with a loan application.
5. Congregational minutes, if necessary, to proceed with a loan application.
6. If applicable, IRS (501)C3 letter of determination. Should your church fall under an "umbrella" exemption from your denominational headquarters, include this information.
7. Current annual report from your state, showing the current status of your church as a corporate entity. (first review to see if you need to update the officers and directors).
8. Deed(s) to church Real Property

Membership Information

Membership and adherent totals should be provided. If available, include a graph demonstrating the growth of the attendance. If the church does not focus on membership numbers, you may want to include sanctuary service attendance(s). Also, provide membership and adherent totals (do not forget to include children). Membership and/or attendance is important to lenders who look for "stable giving units" reflecting ongoing capacity to service a debt.

Biographies of Church Leadership and Staff

In this section, you want to introduce the church or lead pastor(s) and key staff members. Besides the senior pastor, lenders like to see financial support personnel. For example, church business administrator as well as a dedicated bookkeeper. Financial staff holding higher certification or accreditation such as ("CPA") or ("CCA") from The Church Network, as discussed earlier, can be most beneficial.

Philosophy of Debt

I have found some pastors hold different scriptural positions on debt. In this section, describe what the leadership's policy position is on maintaining debt. Some may want to pay it off as soon as practical while others have a high tolerance for it. This helps the lender to understand your philosophy.

Contributions Revenue

The vast majority of churches receive their revenue through individual donations such as tithes and offerings. This can come from their membership and adherents (regular attenders who are not a member) who attend the church but have never joined. Provide information on the number of "giving units" if you have this information combining both members and adherents.

Budget for Current and Past Year

All budgets begin with a philosophy of ministry and focus. How is the money spent in relation to the leadership's mission and purpose? As such, it should be strategic and not simply number crunching or estimating income. Following a well thought out budget assists the leadership to understand how much they plan to spend for each ministry. During the year, you can see if the projected income and expenses are on track. Comparisons with prior years are usually most helpful.

Financial Statements

Important financial reports besides the budget should be included in this document. If you have a CPA, CCA, or bookkeeper, they will help you create these documents. Consider creating the following:

Balance Sheet—This is defined in Black's Law Dictionary 8th Edition as "A statement of an entities' current financial position, disclosing the value of the entities' assets, liabilities, and owners' equity." [24] A balance sheet shows the assets and debts of the church. Be sure to include any real property ownership *information* and current valuations (appraisals if possible) for security of the loan.

---

24 Black, Black's Law Dictionary, 8th Edition, Page 153

Budget—Black's Law Dictionary 8th Edition defines budget as "A statement of an organization's estimated revenues and expenses for a specific period."[25]

Statement of Cash Flows- This shows the churches' sources and uses of donations and other income such as rental income (e.g., cell tower), gift shops, thrift stores, coffee shops, and special events.

Income and Expense Statement—This statement reflects the amount of donations and other income along with details on church expenses.

Donor Restricted Gifts or Funds—This is money held in a trust for a specific purpose.

Your first impression lasts. This packet will help the church present a good first impression.

Everything we have talked about is subject to the will of God and your state law. We serve a mighty God who will help you through the process along with retaining professionals. In the next chapter, we will discuss what to do if the church is sued. A difficult topic but one which is necessary.

Action Points for the Next 30 Days:

1. If your church does not have a balance sheet, create one. If you already have a balance sheet, update it.
2. If you are unaware of your financing opportunities within your denomination, reach out and discover them. Don't assume; ask.
3. In your prayer time, ask the Lord for an opportunity to "expand your stakes" as a church and prepare for something great!
4. Contact the bank your church uses and inquire about a church loan. Know the church's options ahead of time.
5. If your church has lender contacts available now go ahead and discuss what the church is considering. If not, begin securing these contacts.

25 Black, Black's Law Dictionary, 8th Edition, Page 207

CHAPTER

11

Churches and Lawsuits

In this brief chapter, we will discuss the topic of lawsuits. We will address what exactly is a lawsuit, its elements, and what it means to be sued. Then, we will look at what to do if your church is being sued and how to generally prepare for it. It is an uncomfortable topic but a necessary one.

Take all lawsuits seriously and respond to each promptly.

ILLUSTRATION

A pastor called me one day informing me it was his first day at the church. He was going through the previous pastor's desk and found something he wanted to talk to me about. It was a complaint, or a lawsuit, filed and served against the church, still in its envelope in the pastor's desk drawer. Through some investigation, I discovered the church never **answered the complaint** and a default judgment was entered against the church for failing to respond. The new pastor said he couldn't believe discovering this on his first day on the job knowing the previous pastor said nothing to him about it. He then asked me "What can the church do now to fix it?" I helped the new pastor.

Obviously, the lesson here is to not ignore any legal matter. Neglecting to address a complaint does not make it go away; it just makes it worse. Lawsuits are a part of life in our country. As a pastor, if you find yourself or your church being sued, it is not necessarily an indictment on your leadership. Lawsuits happen, and when they do, they must be dealt with.

The first step in suing someone, such as a church, is to file a lawsuit with the county Clerk of Court.

What Does it Mean to be Sued?

"Being sued" basically means a party has filed a lawsuit against you. The lawsuit takes the form of a "pleading" called a complaint or a petition. Black's Law Dictionary defines a pleading as, "A formal document in which a party to a legal proceeding sets forth or responds to allegations, claims, denials or defenses."[26] This critical document is the starting point for the lawsuit and provides the parties and the court with the "cause of action "explaining the dispute between the parties.

What is a "Cause of Action"?

Basically, a lawsuit is a legal grievance. If a party feels it has been wronged, and there has been no resolution, they bring the matter to the court system for justice. The person or party who initiates the lawsuit is called either a plaintiff or a petitioner. The party being sued may be called the defendant or the respondent. This makes up the common parties to the lawsuit.

I will not address third parties who may enter the lawsuit for various legal reasons and rights but suffice it to say in most lawsuits where a church is involved there is an aggrieved party (plaintiff) suing the church (defendant) over a grievance. Examples are many, but here are a few: wrongful termination, sexual molestation of a minor, failure to pay a debt or breach of contract.

Why do Lawsuits Appear in Different Courts?

Most lawsuits churches face land in what lawyers call a "higher court." What this means is the damages sought exceed the minimum amount allowed to appear in that court. Specifically, most U.S. counties have two or three levels of courts: circuit court or superior court, county court, and small claims court. Terminology may differ between states, but these court divisions are common. Each such court has a minimum amount the plaintiff or petitioner must allege to appear in that particular

26 Black, Black's Law Dictionary, 8th Edition, Page 1191

court. For example, with circuit or superior court, the damages involved may have to meet or exceed $15,000 with no maximum. If the plaintiff's damages total $14,000, the circuit court may rule the county court is the proper court to hear the case. For lawsuits involving damages below the county court level, the plaintiff may have to file the lawsuit in the small claims court which is generally a type of county court.

It is important to understand the risk the church faces when it is sued in the highest or circuit/superior court. This is because the lower courts are generally restricted to a maximum amount they can award. For example, if your church is sued in the small claims court, the maximum Judgment the Plaintiff may receive is its award limit or $15,000. But if the church is sued in the highest county court, such as a circuit court, there may not be a maximum award limit. Yes, circuit courts have courts of appeal and supreme courts above them, but typically, these courts hear appeals from lower court findings.

Once you "land in a court," whether it is county or circuit, the plaintiff will petition for a bench or jury trial. In the smaller courts, the judge makes the decision of damages and that is called a bench trial. In higher courts, the petitioner or plaintiff can request a jury trial. As bench trials are common in small claims or county court, jury trials are common in the higher circuit court. With a bench trial, the judge hears the testimony, weighs the evidence, listens to the parties and witnesses, and makes the final judgement or ruling in the case. If the plaintiff wins his case, the judge will issue a judgment for the plaintiff. If it is a defense verdict, the plaintiff may receive nothing. In higher county courts, a jury trial is usually requested. In jury trials, the court or judge makes decisions on law, and the jury makes the decisions of fact. Generally, when the trial is done, it is the jury who decides on an award.

Churches can also be a Plaintiff. Why would a church go to court? The simple answer is to seek legal remedy for a wrong.

What is a Legal Remedy?

When contemplating filing a lawsuit, the main consideration is what can I gain or make right? This is called seeking a legal remedy. Generally speaking, there are four types of remedies that can be awarded by a court in a civil litigation case, and we will discuss each type.

First is the most common remedy: financial damages.

Money damages are typically awarded for negligence and property rights cases. It can also be awarded to an aggrieved employee. It is rare but possible the church can also be responsible for punitive damages used to pay for bad behavior. The allegation may be that the church did something which appears to be "gross negligence." A parting word on financial damages. If allowed in the law, or by contract, the losing party may also have to pay for the successful party's attorney fees and costs.

Second is restitution.

This involves a money award to prevent an unjust enrichment of the defendant. A common example is receiving full payment for a service but not completing the job. Another example may be the court awarding the church a Restitution Judgment against an embezzler for church money stolen.

Third is equitable relief.

This is a nonmonetary damage awarded by the court. Here the plaintiff petitions the court to force a person to stop doing something which violates their civil rights. A common example is when someone petitions the court to issue an injunction to keep someone who is threatening their life to stay away from them. It is also used to force a person to do something they have agreed to do. An example is when a real estate contract fails and one of the two parties' requests "specific performance," which means forcing the defaulting party to complete the transaction.

The final type is declaratory remedy.

This is when someone asks the court for an authoritative determination over a dispute. For example, a church may use this type of remedy when a deed contains a "reverter clause," which means an original owner or someone down the "chain of title" has a claim on the property to go back to them due to a triggering event. An example is when a clause in the deed states the property must be used for a specific purpose and it no longer is. Here, the aggrieved party will ask the court to decide on who is the rightful owner of the property.

Practice Pointer

Be mindful that lawsuits against churches can have various counts or allegations which each can have various remedies including significant economic damages. For example, lawsuits alleging inappropriate touching or molestation of a minor may contain the following counts or allegations: negligence, negligent supervision, negligent hiring/retention, negligent failure to warn, train, or educate, sexual battery, personal injuries, intentional infliction of emotional distress, plus others. The award to the plaintiff if the church is found negligent on one or more counts can be substantial.

Once the plaintiff's attorney has filed the complaint, outlining the allegations against the church and files it with the clerk of court for the county, the next step is to inform the church of the lawsuit so it can answer the allegations. This is when the lawsuit is "served" on the church.

What Does it Mean to be Served a Lawsuit?

Being served a lawsuit is a legal term describing the formal delivery of the lawsuit or complaint. It is a formal action because there must be a "start date and time" when the parties have notice of the lawsuit. Usually, the plaintiff's start date is when the lawsuit is filed, and the defendant's start date is when the complaint is served. This is critical, especially for the defendant or respondent, because there are time limits in order to "answer" the complaint. "Answer" meaning formally responding in writing to the lawsuit. Since it is a formal event, the lawsuit is usually served by a licensed "process server." This is an individual who is authorized to deliver the legal paper to the party named to receive it. While there is a person to serve the lawsuit, there may also be a designated person to receive it. Since churches are nonprofit corporations, the job to receive the complaint falls on the "registered agent."

Registered Agent

A registered agent is a person or corporation who is authorized to accept service of process for someone such as a church corporation. Most state statutes list the obligations of the registered agent such as being present at a certain street address available during business hours to receive such service of process. This has resulted in a cottage industry wherein certain corporations, for an annual fee, agree to act as the church's registered agent.

I find most churches do not designate a professional registered agent but appoint the pastor, a church employee (such as the business administrator), or a board member to act in this capacity. So, what happens if you have been designated as the church's registered agent and a process server serves you a lawsuit? Let's discuss it.

What does our church do if served with a lawsuit?

First, be courteous to the process server. They are only doing their job. Most likely, they have a dozen lawsuits to serve, and it just so happens your church is one of them. They will confirm your identity and hand you the legal papers. Then, the process server having completed the service will write down the date, time and person's name who accepted the service of process. This step establishes "Proof of Service" on the person who accepted the papers. This starts the clock on the timeframes to respond. A process server later informs the Clerk of the Court that service has been provided.

Second, do not ask questions to the process server about the lawsuit or papers. They will most likely not know any details about the lawsuit or why it was filed, so asking them questions about it will not assist you.

Third, make a copy of the papers you were served so in case you misplace it another copy exists.

Fourth, pull the church's liability insurance policy and contact your agent. Inform the agent you have been served and request they notify the liability carrier giving them formal notification of the service of process. It is important to secure written verification from the insurance company that you have given them prompt notice of the lawsuit. Failure to do so may result in loss of coverage or a Reservation of Rights letter.

Fifth, call your church attorney informing them of what just took place. Keep in mind the liability carrier may provide the church with legal representation. More on that a little later.

Sixth, open a file for this matter and gather whatever documents you can to assist the attorney who will represent the church. Your insurance defense attorney will want to discuss this lawsuit in detail and the more information they have helps in preparing the church's answer to the complaint. If the church does not file a written answer or response within the time frame contained in the summons or follow the instructions the summons states, the plaintiff may proceed anyway, and the church may end up admitting the allegations by not responding and having a default judgement entered against the church. So timely preparation and assistance with your insurance carrier and legal counsel will go a long way.

Finally, and most importantly, have the church defense counsel answer or respond to the lawsuit. I do not recommend doing it yourself.

Benefit of liability insurance coverage

Assuming the church has liability insurance to cover the claim associated with the lawsuit, in most cases, the insurance company will secure legal representation for the church. The good news about this is the lawyer services will most likely be paid for through the insurance liability policy. This is often good news, not just because of the money saved but because insurance companies have business relationships with excellent law firms. Securing excellent and experienced counsel to defend the church is therefore likely.

Keep in mind the available limits of coverage may decrease as the insurance pays for the church's attorney. There are cases where because the attorney fees will exceed the policy limits the insurance carrier will tender or pay the limits to get out of the case.

Securing legal counsel when there is no liability insurance coverage

Assuming the church does not have liability insurance to cover the claim associated with the lawsuit, the church is on its own to hire legal counsel and pay for their services. This can be very costly. Trial work is stressful, and litigators charge commensurate rates. But the expense is necessary to preserve the church's legal rights.

Action Points for the Next 30 Days:

1. Assuming your church has general liability insurance, review your coverage to ensure your church's activities are insured.
2. If your church has no church attorney, begin searching for one to give general assistance and guidance on legal matters with the church. If a lawsuit is

filed and there is no liability insurance, your church attorney will represent the church or refer you to another litigator to represent its interests.

3. Insufficient legal counsel or liability coverage can expose your church to liabilities. Begin budgeting accordingly.

CHAPTER

12

Dissolving the Church

"To everything there is a season.... a time to be born, and a time to die...."

Ecclesiastes 3:1,2

One day, I received a call from a senior pastor saying he had been serving the congregation for many years and felt the Lord had directed him to dissolve the church. When I asked him why, he said the membership had dwindled to a few people, and he felt the Holy Spirit was directing him to an out-of-state ministry. When I asked him how the finances were, he told me they were fine. I did not expect that answer since in most cases, when the membership dwindles, the donations dry up. In fact, he said "John, I will need your help with finances." I said, "How so?" He said, "We have close to a million dollars in our operating account, without any debt, and I need your help on how and where to legally give it away." I did just that for him along with dissolving his entity.

The dissolution of a church is not only a legal process but also a very emotional process for those involved. It is often viewed as an "ending of a ministry," but it does not have to be. Several of the churches I have represented for dissolution were resurrected by the Lord albeit under a different name, although most never restart.

In this chapter, we will discuss the reasons why churches dissolve and then address the process for dissolution.

What is Dissolution?

Black's Law Dictionary defines corporate dissolution as "A corporation whose charter has expired or been revoked, relinquished, or voluntarily terminated."[27] As we discussed in Chapter Two on incorporation when a Charter or Articles of Incorporation are filed with the state, the corporate entity is birthed and comes into existence. The termination of such a Charter or Articles then renders the corporation dissolved.

But what makes a church or corporate entity dissolve? If it is true when Jesus said, "I will build My church and the gates of Hell shall not prevail against it." (Matthew 16:18), then why do church corporations dissolve? First, realize we will not be discussing the ongoing existence of the universal church or its people as Jesus was referencing, but the corporate entity created by His church and subsequently dissolved through the state.

There are several reasons why dissolution of a church happens. Let us briefly look at them.

Common Causes for Dissolution

Over the years, I have found dissolution falls into two categories: voluntary and involuntary. Let us first address voluntary dissolution.

Voluntary Dissolution

With voluntary dissolution, the church's leadership and/or members decide to dissolve the church. This can happen for several reasons, but in my experience, the most common reason churches "fold" or "dissolve" is for economic reasons.

Economic Reasons

Dissolution can occur when a church is sued, loses the case, and it had no liability insurance or was covered but judgment exceeded the policy limits. But most of the time it is not because of a lawsuit but for difficulty paying bills, and after a period of struggling, they decide and vote to dissolve. The loss of tithes or donations can

27 Garner, Black's Law Dictionary, 8th Edition, 366

result from several factors. Among them can be general economic conditions such as the local economy. Many churches operate with little margin or savings. Often leadership operates by spending virtually every cent which comes in and failing to plan for the lean years. This is often disguised as "operating in faith" and not planning as the bible instructs us to do. Although I do not find faith and planning/budgeting a margin as incompatible, unfortunately some church leaders do.

Besides economic conditions, another common reason is a loss of membership.

Loss of Membership

This directly impacts revenue. It is obvious when you lose members you lose contributors or tithers. When this happens, the church has a reduction in revenue but not a reduction in expenses. That may be because many of the church's expenses are "fixed" or are a monthly obligation. The reasons why church members leave a church are varied; inability to make friends, doctrinal differences, apathy, and "in-fighting" are common reasons. In my experience, the failure, or the voluntary leaving, of the senior pastor will most likely result in a loss of people thus income.

Loss of Senior Pastor

The loss of a church's senior or lead pastor or minister can also have a serious negative financial effect upon a church. This can happen in several ways: moral failure of the pastor, deciding to pastor another church, voluntary retirement, or termination of employment. Whatever the reason, when there is this type of transition, it is not uncommon for the membership to react negatively in some way, with families leaving the church.

General Attrition

Since Covid there has been (currently) a noticeable loss of attendance in the churches across our country. The reduction in membership has been attributed to families continuing to stay home post pandemic. Additionally, many in the Gen Z and Millennial generation have a negative view on the "formal institution" of the church. These two factors have caused a noticeable drop in attendance and/or slower growth in churches across our county. Thus, causing a negative fiscal impact.

Charlie Kirk Effect

The tragic assassination of Charlie Kirk has caused an increase of young people to attend church. It is too early to tell if this is a short or long term phenomenon. But this author believes it has the potential of changing the current trend of church attendance for the better.

In sum, the above-mentioned causes and others have resulted in churches needing to dissolve. But before I discuss the process for voluntary dissolution, we need first to address the occasional occurrence of involuntary dissolution and its consequences. Yes, churches dissolve without the leadership knowing.

Administrative or Involuntary Dissolution

Each state requires nonprofit corporations to be in compliance with the state nonprofit corporation law under which it was organized. When there is noncompliance with certain filing requirements "administrative" dissolution may be the result.

There are several reasons why a state may administratively dissolve a nonprofit. Common reasons are as follows. First, operating without a registered agent. This is a designated person or corporation to receive service of process on the entity. Second, failure to notify the state of the change of address for the registered agent. Third, failure to timely respond to inquiries by the state on the status of the corporation. Fourth, the corporation's period of duration has ended. Although most nonprofits list their period of duration "perpetual," some do not. In one church I helped their Articles of Incorporation stated the period of duration for the church corporation was "through the life of the final surviving incorporator." Finally, the corporation failed to file its annual report and pay the filing fee before the due date plus any days of grace offered by the state to do so. In this report, are the names of the officers, directors, and the registered agent for the corporation.

Failure to file this report may result in the involuntary or "administrative" dissolution of the corporation. This can result in the Articles of Incorporation being administratively dissolved, revoked, or forfeited and a "Certificate of Dissolution" being issued. The terminology may be different between states, but the result is the same. The nonprofit corporation then ceases to exist under state law.

Process for administrative dissolution may include a "Notice of Intent to Dissolve" by the state. Usually, this notice comes with a time to "cure" or fix the possible oversight. I say possible because sometimes an attorney encourages the client to administratively dissolve and not voluntarily dissolve since there is usually no cost to the client for administrative dissolution and no attorney fees. However, there are risks for the corporate officers and directors to involuntarily dissolve to avoid paying such fees and costs.

If the corporation does not fix or cure the "Notice of Intent to Dissolve" there are serious implications for nonprofits if this occurs. First, although the corporation may continue to exist it may not conduct any affairs except what is necessary to wind up and liquidate its affairs. Second, in Florida, a director, officer, or agent who knows the corporation is administratively dissolved and proposes to act on behalf of the corporation may be "personally liable for the debts, obligations, and liabilities of the corporation arising from such action and incurred subsequent to the corporation's administrative dissolution." Florida Statute 617.1421

Besides the personal liability of the director and officer, there is also a significant risk to the entity itself.

Risk of Loss of Tax Exemption Due to Involuntary Dissolution

Another major risk the church faces by involuntary dissolution with its state of incorporation is the risk of losing its tax-exempt status with the Internal Revenue Service (IRS). To illustrate this, let us look at IRS Private Letter Ruling (PLR) on this topic.

PLR 202242011

A Private Letter Ruling is a written statement sent from the IRS to a taxpayer which applies tax laws to a particular situation. The IRS charges a fee for this letter. Here, a nonprofit organization lost its tax exemption because the secretary of state revoked its corporate charter for failing to update and file their annual report. Specifically, a charity filed for its 501(c)(3) and during the pre-contact planning phase of investigation a revenue agent found out its corporate status with its state had been revoked. This was discovered when the IRS agent looked at the state's website. Although the IRS agent made several attempts to reach out to the nonprofit on this issue, requesting "proof that it is in good standing with the state of incorporation" none was provided.

The IRS concluded, for this and other reasons, its tax-exempt status under section 501©(3) should be revoked. (See Appendix 3).

The lesson here is clear. First, complete the annual report maintaining the church status as current. Second, when contacted by the IRS, answer their questions. I can only speculate that this nonprofit had no idea that by not filing their annual report their exempt status would be revoked. But it was. This should not have happened. Correcting such a legal defect is common practice.

What happens if a church finds its Articles of Incorporation or Charter revoked, dissolved, or forfeited? The first step is to speak with an attorney, and a CPA, if necessary, to determine the feasibility of "reinstatement" to current status. What is involved in reinstating a dissolved nonprofit entity? Glad you asked. Let us look at three states, Florida, Texas, and New York statutes to see how they handle reinstatement of an administratively dissolved nonprofit entity.

Reinstatement of an Administratively Dissolved Corporation under Three States

Comment: Keep in mind, not all the statutory language is cited due to space. To address this issue in totality, have your legal counsel pull up the full statute in your state of incorporation for review and consultation. Let's now look at Florida.

Bold, italicized is my emphasis.

Florida Reinstatement Following Administrative Dissolution.

"(1) A corporation administratively dissolved under s. 617.1421 ***may apply*** *to the department for reinstatement at any time after the effective date of dissolution. The corporation* ***must submit a reinstatement form*** *prescribed and furnished by the department or a current uniform business report signed by a registered agent and an officer or director and* ***submit all fees*** *owed by the corporation and computed at the rate provided by law at the time the corporation applies for reinstatement.*

(2) If the department determines that the application contains the information required by subsection (1) and that the information is correct, it ***shall reinstate*** *the corporation.*

(4) ***The name of the dissolved corporation is not available for assumption*** *or use by another corporation until 1 year after the effective date of dissolution* ***unless*** *the dissolved corporation provides the department with an affidavit*

executed pursuant to s. 617.01201 authorizing the immediate assumption or use of the name by another corporation.

(5) *If the name of the dissolved corporation has been lawfully assumed in this state by another corporation, the department shall require the dissolved corporation to* ***amend its articles of incorporation to change its name*** *before accepting its application for reinstatement."*

Losing the church's name would be unfortunate. Texas also has a similar provision for reinstatement.

Texas Reinstatement Following Administrative Dissolution.

Texas Statute § 22.365

Bold, italicized is my emphasis.

a) *"A corporation that is terminated or the registration of which has been revoked as provided by Section 22.364 may be relieved of the termination or revocation by* ***filing the report*** *required by Section 22.357, accompanied by the filing fee for the report, if the corporation has paid....*

b) "When the report is filed and the filing fee is paid to the secretary of state, the secretary of state ***shall:(1) reinstate the certificate of Formation or registration without judicial action...."***

The Texas statute is similar to Florida in that the corporation may lose its name.

c) ***"If*** *a termination or revocation is set aside under this section, the corporation shall determine from the secretary of state* ***whether the name of the corporation is available.*** *If the name of the corporation is* ***not*** *available at the time of reinstatement, the corporation* ***shall amend its corporate name*** *under this code."*

Finally, let's look at New York who has similar provisions although they call it "dissolution by proclamation."

New York Reinstatement Following Administrative Dissolution.

New York NPC § 1014. Dissolution of Domestic Corporations by Proclamation:

Bold, italicized is my emphasis.

"Every corporation incorporated pursuant to this chapter, other than a corporation incorporated pursuant to article 15 (Public cemetery corporations), and registered or required to be registered pursuant to article 7-A of the executive law or article 8 of the estates, powers and trusts law ***shall be subject to dissolution for failure to register or to file annual financial reports*** in accordance with the following procedures:

(a) *"On or before the last day of March, June, September and December in each calendar year, the attorney general may certify and transmit to the department of state a list containing the names of any or all corporations...* ***that have not filed annual financial reports*** *for each of the* ***five years*** *immediately preceding the date of such certification. This section shall not be applicable to corporations that filed reports deemed by the attorney general to be incomplete, erroneous or otherwise deficient.*

b) "No corporation shall be included in any list prepared pursuant to paragraph (a) of this section unless (1) in each of the last ***two years*** *during which such corporation failed to file its annual report, the attorney general has sent to such corporation* ***by certified mail return receipt requested notice that the corporation has failed to file*** *and has three months from the date of such notice to file all delinquent reports and complete all registration requirements... .*

(d) The secretary of state shall make a proclamation under his or her hand and seal of office as to each list received from the attorney general declaring any corporations whose names are included in such list ***to be dissolved and their certificates of incorporation to be forfeited****.*

e) "Upon the publication of such proclamation in the manner proscribed in paragraph (d) of this section, ***each corporation named therein shall be deemed dissolved without further legal proceedings.***

(h) "Any corporation so dissolved ***may file in the department of state a written consent by the attorney general to the reinstatement of the corporation.*** *Such written consent shall be given if the attorney general shall have received all annual financial reports and fees required by article 7-A of the executive law and article 8 of the estates, powers and trusts law and penalties and interest charges related thereto have been paid or waived. The filing of such consent shall have the effect of* ***annulling*** *all of the proceedings theretofore*

taken under the provisions of this section for the dissolution of such corporation with the same force and effect ***as if such proclamation had not been made or published.*** *The fee of the secretary of state for filing such consent shall be fifty dollars.* ***No such consent shall be filed if*** *the name of a domestic not-for-profit corporation, business corporation, not-for-profit corporation, limited liability company or limited partnership formed later than one year after the publication of the proclamation of dissolution, or the name or fictitious name or of a foreign business corporation, not-for-profit corporation, limited liability company or limited partnership which has obtained authority to do business or conduct activities in the state later than one year after such proclamation,* ***or name which has been reserved later than one year after such proclamation,*** *is the same as or may not be distinguished from the name of the corporation filing such consent unless such corporation simultaneously files in the department of state a certificate of amendment to change the name of such corporation. Such certificate of amendment shall be executed in a manner as if such corporation had not been dissolved.*

(j) "Whenever a corporation shall have complied with paragraph (h) of this section or whenever the procedures specified in paragraph (i) of this section shall have been taken, the secretary of state shall publish a notice thereof in the state register and shall send a copy of such notice to the county clerk of the county in which, according to his or her records, the office of the corporation is located. Such county clerk shall file such copy and make appropriate entry on his or her records without charge." "

In summary, all three states—Florida, Texas, and New York—provide methods to fix or cure the involuntary dissolution. Although allowing it to happen has risks, such as the loss of the corporate name and possibly its IRS exemption. But what if the corporation decides to voluntarily dissolve? We will discuss this next.

Voluntary Dissolution.

A nonprofit can decide itself to dissolve. The voluntary dissolution of a church corporation requires the nonprofit to follow the laws of the state of incorporation on the process to dissolve. Since laws differ in each state it is imperative to secure the legal services of a competent nonprofit attorney to guide the church through such a process. The following represents what I have found to be a customary practice to follow in dissolving a church.

Board of Directors Resolution Approving Dissolution

The dissolution process begins with the governing authority approving the dissolution of the corporation which generally means the board of directors. Some states clearly outline what this Resolution must say approving the dissolution. The next question is "does the church membership need to vote on dissolution?"

Membership Resolution Approving Dissolution

Here the church governing documents or state law requires a vote of the membership. If it does, then consider calling for a membership business meeting for the special purpose of voting to dissolve the entity. Make sure the meeting has proper notice, quorum and be prepared to discuss the reasons why it is necessary. Be mindful, some states require a certain percentage of members to approve a dissolution. Whoever votes and approves the dissolution is guided by the church's governing documents and then the incorporating states statutes.

For example, in **Florida**, a majority of the board of directors is required. Additionally, If the membership is required to vote then at least a majority of them must also approve a resolution to dissolve.

Bold, italicized is my emphasis

617.1402 ***Dissolution of corporation.*** *A corporation desiring to dissolve and wind up its affairs must adopt a resolution to dissolve in the following manner:*

(1) ***"If the corporation has members entitled to vote on a resolution to dissolve****, and unless the board of directors determines that because of a conflict of interest or other substantial reason it should not make any recommendation, the board of directors must adopt a resolution recommending that the corporation be dissolved and* ***directing that the question of such dissolution be submitted to a vote at a meeting of members entitled to vote thereon,*** *which may be either an annual or special meeting. Written notice stating that the purpose, or one of the purposes, of such meeting is to consider the advisability of dissolving the corporation must be given to each member entitled to vote at such meeting in accordance with the articles of incorporation or the bylaws. A resolution to dissolve the corporation shall be adopted upon receiving* ***at least a majority*** *of the votes which members present at such meeting or represented by proxy are entitled to cast.*

(2) ***If the corporation has no members or if its members are not entitled to vote on a resolution to dissolve,*** *the dissolution of the corporation may be authorized at a meeting of the board of directors by a* ***majority vote*** *of the directors then in office."*

Any vote required by the directors or members to dissolve should be set forth in the governing documents such as the articles of incorporation, constitution, or bylaws, or if not, the statutory default rule governs. Many church governing documents follow the prescribed language provided by the IRS for dissolving a nonprofit entity thus satisfying their "organizational test."

IRS Language in Governing Documents

Satisfying the IRS Organizational Test

As we discussed earlier, a requirement for approval by the IRS as an exempt entity is for the nonprofit to have a dissolution paragraph in the articles of incorporation which is part of the organizational test.

Section 1.501(c)(3)-1(b)(4) of the regulations states that an organization is not organized exclusively for one or more exempt purposes unless its assets are dedicated to an exempt purpose. An organization's assets will be considered dedicated to an exempt purpose, if upon dissolution, such assets would by reason of a provision in the organization's articles or by operation of law, be distributed for one or more exempt purposes.

IRS Suggested Articles of Incorporation Dissolution Language

"The IRS provides the following suggested language to use:

Upon the dissolution of the corporation, assets shall be distributed for one or more exempt purposes within the meaning of section 501(c)(3) of the Internal Revenue Code, or the corresponding section of any future federal tax code, or shall be distributed to the federal government, or to a state or local government, for a public purpose. Any such assets not so disposed of shall be disposed of by a Court of Competent Jurisdiction of the county in which the principal office of the corporation is then located, exclusively for such purposes or to such organization or organizations, as said Court shall determine, which are organized and operated exclusively for such purposes."

IRS Website: Life Cycle of a Public Charity.

Plan of Dissolution of Assets

After dissolution is approved, the church may continue to exist BUT solely to wind up its affairs, liquidate its assets, pay debts, and distribute any remaining assets. This can be a very emotional time. Exactly what the entity does with its remaining assets can be controversial. Although implemented later, I highly suggest working on this issue early in the process since questions about remaining assets will most likely be raised. The "natives" or families who have been in the church and invested much of their time and money (tithes) want to know where the church's money and property goes upon dissolution.

As such, a carefully drafted plan of distribution must be laid out to outline the remaining assets and who is to receive them. It is highly suggested the church secures the services of a nonprofit CPA and attorney to assist in the area.

As mentioned in the required IRS language, the assets must go to another nonprofit entity. If the dissolving entity is a 501(c) (3) organization, it is required by federal tax law to distribute its remaining assets for tax-exempt status purposes, such as by distributing the assets to another 501(c) (3) organization. The dissolving church needs to verify that any entity receiving church resources is also not only incorporated as nonprofit but is also an exempt entity and eligible to receive the assets. A dissolving church may request their letter of determination from the IRS verifying this, if available. Churches are not obligated to file for their exemption if they operate under the IRS's definition of a "church." Remember? Additionally, the recipient entity should be similar in purpose and beliefs. Verifying their eligibility is important to comply with the IRS language of dissolution. If the receiving ministry of the assets is not a church but a "ministry" I require them to produce to our office their exemption "Letter of Determination," otherwise no money!

Articles of Dissolution

Articles of dissolution must be filed with the incorporating state for dissolution to be effective. Depending upon the state, this filing may be made any time after dissolution is approved, or it may have to be made after the winding up and distribution of assets is completed. Each state has its own requirements.

Filing Articles of Dissolution with the State of Incorporation

After the board of directors (also the membership if required), approve the dissolution and the associated plan of distribution and any other state required activity the nonprofit files its dissolution with the State of Incorporation.

In many cases, the corporation continues to exist but solely to wind up its affairs, liquidate its assets, pay outstanding debts, and distribute any remaining assets. The winding-up period includes, among other steps,

- withdrawing from the states where the nonprofit corporation was qualified to do business
- canceling licenses and registrations
- notifying and paying creditors, employees, clients, and donors

Depending upon the state, this filing may be made any time after dissolution is approved, or it may have to be made after the winding up and distribution of assets is completed. Again, seek professional legal counsel in your state to guide you as to its requirements.

State Notification of Dissolution and Tax Clearance

The nonprofit may also be required to file a tax clearance certificate. This is a certificate from the state tax department stating that the nonprofit corporation does not owe the state any taxes or reports. Some states require notification of, or approval by, other state officials such as the attorney general.

IRS Notification of Dissolution

Finally, assuming the church has followed the state requirements, we will now discuss notifying the IRS of the dissolution. What organizations have to notify the IRS, and which do not? If required, what must be done? Also, who should be doing this? I suggest the church retain a competent CPA to determine if filing is required and/or to draft any documents to file notifying the IRS of the dissolution.

Internal Revenue Code Section 6043(b) and Treasury Regulations Section 1.6043-3 establish rules for when a tax-exempt organization must notify the IRS that it has undergone a liquidation, dissolution, or termination. As a general rule, most organizations must notify the IRS when they terminate or dissolve.

If the church is included on the Master File for Exempt Organizations, notice of dissolution will remove the organization from that listing.

Keep in mind the IRS may require the following documents to be included in your notice.

- Articles of dissolution filed with the state of incorporation.

- Minutes of the meeting of directors and/or membership, signed by a corporate officer, of the vote to dissolve.
- Resolution to dissolve a trust, signed and dated by a trustee if the entity is an unincorporated association. (A church not incorporated, remember?)
- A list of the last directors, trustees, or officers, with their contact information.
- Plan of distribution of assets of the dissolving entity.

If you did not file for tax-exempt status with the IRS because the entity was affiliated with a parent organization that holds a group exemption number, the entity should provide the parent organization with the above information. Allow the church's CPA to guide you on what is required and necessary.

Conclusion

Closing the doors of any church is never easy, especially after many godly people have poured their heart, soul, and finances for its success. If the decision to dissolve is made first, consider preparing a plan to distribute the remaining assets rights away. Review the entities governing documents to verify who must vote and approve the dissolution. Be mindful that the proper filing of the dissolution documents with the state of incorporation and the IRS is critical. Careful consideration is suggested in making the decision to dissolve and proceeding from the start with the assistance and guidance of a nonprofit attorney and CPA.

Action Points for the Next 30 Days:

1. Do your policies account for timely filing and annual reporting required by your state of incorporation? If not, create the necessary guidance.
2. Review and adhere to your church's articles of incorporation dissolution language. Review the church's constitution and bylaws for language regarding dissolution.
3. Determine a distribution model for your church's assets in the case of dissolution. Verify the recipient nonprofit's eligibility and alignment with your nonprofit's beliefs, purpose, and vision.
4. Secure a competent nonprofit attorney and CPA if your considering dissolving your church.

Conclusion

In this book, we have discussed many legal issues involved from creating, maintaining, and dissolving a church. Topics such as formal legal incorporation, governance, taxes, records, personnel, specific legal risks, real estate, financing, and lawsuits through dissolution have been addressed.

A well-run, organized church can last for decades, even centuries. My prayer is that this book has assisted you and your church. If it has, would you please consider emailing me how it has? Contact me at churchlawbook@gmail.com

This should "tie a bow" on our time together. I want to say thank you for reading my book. My prayer is that it has blessed you and your church. Remember this book only offers legal information and not advice. Secure the services of a competent nonprofit attorney in your state to advise and guide you through all of your church's legal issues.

Also, have a competent nonprofit CPA to guide the church in tax and IRS issues.

Allow me in these concluding thoughts to highlight certain key items/tasks for you to consider for your church. You can check them off once done.

Does your charter or articles of incorporation satisfy the IRS organizational and operational tests as an exempt entity?

The *Organization Test* requires the entity to be organized exclusively for exempt purposes, as specified in IRC Section 501(c)(3). The *Operational Test* examines whether the organization primarily engages in activities that further its exempt purposes.

If your documents do not have such language, secure the services of a nonprofit attorney to **review and seek advice on amending accordingly.**

Does your governing board understand and operate with a duty of loyalty?
This duty requires directors to use their authority only in good faith. This duty also involves holding matters in confidence and acting in the best interest of the organization.

Does your governing board understand and operate with a duty of care?
This duty calls upon directors to act in an informed and reasonable manner when deciding matters and in the corresponding management of the church.

Does your governing board understand and operate with a duty of obedience?
This duty calls upon directors to act and follow the church's governing documents. If necessary, also your state's nonprofit law.

Does your governing board operate under a written conflict of interest policy?
A typical conflict of interest policy will address the following:
What circumstances qualify as a conflict of interest?
How should the board handle conflict when they arise?
What, if any, role can the conflicted board members have?
The process for resolving such conflicts.

Does your church have a written record retention policy?
Consider it as a document management strategy for your nonprofit. It is important because it is unrealistic to expect all records to be preserved indefinitely. Such a policy will provide clear guidance to your staff on exactly what to keep and discard.

Does your church screen all volunteers and employees who work with minors and continue to do so on a consistent basis?
This is critical to avoid a tragedy occurring both to a child and the church.

Does your church conduct an annual evaluation of its employees?
First, this addresses the work performance of the employee. Second, it allows the employees to receive feedback on their management performance. Third, it allows

the employer to fix performance deficiencies before they get out of hand and/or require termination. Fourth, it gives the employer an opportunity to express undiscovered skills/values unknown to the employee. Finally, it may protect the church in case there are allegations of wrongful or no-cause termination, discrimination, and the like.

Does your church have in place written internal financial controls in place to prevent theft or embezzlement?
It is so important to have a group of trusting people who rotate functions to handle donations.

Does your church lease its property only to other nonprofits with a similar exempt purpose or has it unknowingly leased to for-profit entities?
Pull out all leases the church has entered into and investigate their entity status.

Does your church liability insurance policy have proper coverage to protect your church and its directors and officers?
If you're not sure, meet with your liability insurance agent and ask them to review and make suggestions for further protection(s) for your church. This may include sexual molestation coverage, wrongful termination, error, and omissions, etc.

Does your church currently own real estate?
If so, how is the property titled? Is it properly titled in the legal corporate name of the nonprofit?

Does your church have a current balance sheet showing the assets and liabilities of the organization?
Knowing the current financial condition prevents the leadership from making bad financial decisions.

Does your church have someone in charge of filing any annual reporting required by your state of incorporation to avoid involuntary dissolution?
If not, go ahead and appoint someone to do this important job.

Does your church have a competent nonprofit attorney and CPA to help guide you in all these areas we have discussed?

If not, proceed to retain such professionals.

God bless you and His Church,

John Joseph

P.S. If my book has in any way helped your church would you please inform your fellow ministers and leadership of this book and email me at churchlawbook@gmail.com and let me know?

My website address is www.churchlegalcenter.com
In Him,
John

Appendix # 1

Private Letter Rulings from the Internal Revenue Service.

IRS
Department of the Treasury
Internal Revenue Service
Tax Exempt and Government Entities
PO Box 2508
Cincinnati, OH 45201

Date:
November 10, 2020
Employer ID number:

Form you must file:

Tax years:

Person to contact:
Name:
ID number:
Telephone:

Number: 202105009
Release Date: 2/5/2021

UIL: 501.00-00, 501.03-05, 501.03-30

Dear :

This letter is our final determination that you don't qualify for exemption from federal income tax under Internal Revenue Code (IRC) Section 501(a) as an organization described in IRC Section 501(c)(3). Recently, we sent you a proposed adverse determination in response to your application. The proposed adverse determination explained the facts, law, and basis for our conclusion, and it gave you 30 days to file a protest. Because we didn't receive a protest within the required 30 days, the proposed determination is now final.

Because you don't qualify as a tax-exempt organization under IRC Section 501(c)(3), donors generally can't deduct contributions to you under IRC Section 170.

We may notify the appropriate state officials of our determination, as required by IRC Section 6104(c), by sending them a copy of this final letter along with the proposed determi tion letter.

You must file the federal income tax forms for the tax years shown above within **30 days** from the date of this letter unless you request an extension of time to file. For further instructions, forms, and information, visit www.irs.gov.

We'll make this final adverse determination letter and the proposed adverse determination letter available for public inspection after deleting certain identifying information, as required by IRC Section 6110. Read the enclosed Notice 437, Notice of Intention to Disclose, and review the two attached letters that show our proposed deletions. If you disagree with our proposed deletions, follow the instructions in the Notice 437 on how to notify us. If you agree with our deletions, you don't need to take any further action.

If you have questions about this letter, you can call the contact person shown above. If you have questions about your federal income tax status and responsibilities, call our customer service number at 800-829-1040 (TTY 800-829-4933 for deaf or hard of hearing) or customer service for businesses at 800-829-4933.

Sincerely,

Stephen A. Martin
Director, Exempt Organizations
Rulings and Agreements

Enclosures:
Notice 437
Redacted Letter 4034
Redacted Letter 4038

Letter 4038 (Rev. 5-2020)
Catalog Number 47632S

IRS

Department of the Treasury
Internal Revenue Service
P.O. Box 2508
Cincinnati, OH 45201

Date:
September 8, 2020
Employer ID number:

Contact person/ID number:

Contact telephone number:

Contact fax number:

UIL:
501.00-00
501.03-05
501.03-30

Legend:
M = Date
N = State
P = Number
Q = Number

Dear :

We considered your application for recognition of exemption from federal income tax under Internal Revenue Code (IRC) Section 501(a). We determined that you don't qualify for exemption under IRC Section 501(c)(3). This letter explains the reasons for our conclusion. Please keep it for your records.

Issues
Do you qualify for exemption under IRC Section 501(c)(3)? No, for the reasons stated below.

Facts
You submitted Form 1023-EZ, Streamline Application for Recognition of Exemption Under Section 501(c)(3) of the Internal Revenue Code. You attest that you have the necessary organizing document, that your organizing document limits your purposes to one or more exempt purposes within the meaning of IRC Section 501(c)(3), that your organizing document does not expressly empower you to engage in activities, other than an insubstantial part, that are not in furtherance of one or more exempt purposes, and that your organizing document contains the dissolution provision required under Section 501(c)(3). You further attest that you are organized and operated exclusively to further charitable purposes and that you have not conducted and will not conduct prohibited activities under Section 501(c)(3).

Your stated mission or most significant activities on Form 1023-EZ were described as "women's softball team." During review of your Form 1023-EZ, detailed information was requested supplemental to your attestations. You were incorporated on M in the state of N. Your Articles of Incorporation are silent regarding your purpose or how you will dispose of your assets upon dissolution.

Letter 4034 (Rev. 11-2018)
Catalog Number 47628K

2

You describe yourself as a softball team that plays in tournaments, usually once a month. The age group of your players are adults between P and Q years old.

You do not conduct fundraising. You rely on advertising funds received from businesses. The name(s) of the business(es) will be on your uniforms and seen everywhere you play.

Law

IRC Section 501(c)(3) provides for the recognition of exemption of organizations that are organized and operated exclusively for religious, charitable or other purposes as specified in the statute. No part of the net earnings may inure to the benefit of any private shareholder or individual.

Treasury Regulation Section 1.501(c)(3)-1(a)(1) states that, in order to be exempt as an organization described in IRC Section 501(c)(3), an organization must be both organized and operated exclusively for one or more of the purposes specified in such section. If an organization fails to meet either the organizational test or the operational test, it is not exempt.

Treas. Reg. Section 1.501(c)(3)-1(b)(1)(i) provides that an organization is organized exclusively for one or more exempt purposes only if its articles of organization limit the purposes of such organization to one or more exempt purposes and do not expressly empower the organization engage, otherwise than as an insubstantial part of its activities, in activities that in themselves are not in furtherance of one or more exempt purposes.

Treas. Reg. Section 1.501(c)(3)-l(b)(4) holds that an organization is not organized exclusively for one or more exempt purposes unless its assets are dedicated to an exempt purpose. An organization's assets will be considered dedicated to an exempt purpose, for example, if, upon dissolution, such assets would, by reason of a provision in the organization's articles or operation of law, be distributed for one or more exempt purposes.

Treas. Reg. Section 1.501(c)(3)-1(c)(1) provides that an organization will be regarded as operated exclusively for one or more exempt purposes only if it engages primarily in activities which accomplish one or more of such exempt purposes specified in IRC Section 501(c)(3). An organization will not be so regarded if more than an insubstantial part of its activities is not in furtherance of an exempt purpose.

Revenue Ruling 64-275,1964-2 C.B. 142, held an organization formed for the purpose of training suitable candidates in the techniques of racing sailboats in national and international competition, and thereby improving the caliber of candidates representing the United States in Olympic and Pan-American games, qualifies for exemption as an educational organization described in IRC Section 501(c)(3).

Rev. Rul. 65-2, 1965-1 C.B. 227, describes an organization that is organized and operated for the purpose of teaching a particular sport to children under the ages of 18 by holding clinics conducted by qualified instructors. The organization was described in IRC Section 501(c)(3) because it is exclusively charitable and educational.

Rev. Rul. 70-4, 1970-1 C.B. 126, describes an organization engaged in promoting and regulating a sport for amateurs. Their stated purposes were to promote the health of the general public by encouraging all persons to improve their physical condition and fostering public interest in a particular sport. Its activities were directed toward promoting sport tournaments, exhibitions and holding instructive clinics. The organization did not qualify for exemption under IRC Section 501(c)(3).

3

Rev. Rul. 80-215, 1980-2 C.B. 174, describes an organization that was formed to develop, promote and regulate a sport for youth under the ages of 18 and to promote sportsmanlike competition among the players. It also promulgated rules, organized officials, and presented seminars for players and coaches and referees. The organization combatted juvenile delinquency by providing a recreational outlet for the young people, which is a charitable purpose. Furthermore, the organization was educational because it developed the skills of the youth.

In Better Business Bureau of Washington, D.C., Inc. v. United States, 326 U.S. 279 (1945), the Supreme Court determined the activities of that organization were aimed at promoting the prosperity and standing of the business community and therefore, served a substantial private purpose. It concluded that the presence of a single nonexempt purpose, if substantial in nature, will preclude exemption regardless of the number or importance of statutorily exempt purposes.

In Hutchinson Baseball Enterprises, Inc. v. Commissioner, 696 F.2d. 757 (1982), the court held that an organization that promoted recreational and amateur sports was exempt as a charitable organization under IRC Section 501(c)(3). The organization undertook numerous activities to promote the sport of baseball and the court found that the purpose of promoting sports predominated over subsidiary purposes, such as members' recreational or social benefit.

In Media Sports League, Inc. v. Commissioner, T.C. Memo 1986-568 (1986), the court ruled that an organization that sponsored sports competitions for adults in the community was not exempt under IRC Section 501 (c)(3). The court found that the organization had the substantial nonexempt purpose of promoting the social and recreational interests of its members.

In Wayne Baseball, Inc. v. Commissioner, T.C. Memo. 1999-304 (1999), the court held that the organization's nonexempt social and recreational activities were substantial in comparison to the organization's promotion of baseball in the community. The Court found that the only activity sponsored by the organization was the operation of an adult amateur baseball team and that the primary beneficiaries of the organization were the individual team participants.

Application of law

IRC Section 501(c)(3) and Treas. Reg. Section 1.501(c)(3)-1(a)(1) set forth two main tests to qualify for exempt status. An organization must be both organized and operated exclusively for purposes described in Section 501(c)(3). You have failed to meet both requirements, as explained below.

Your Articles of Incorporation includes no stated purpose. Because your organizing document does not limit your purposes to exclusively IRC Section 501(c)(3) purposes, you do not meet the requirements of Treas. Reg. Section 1.501 (c)(3)-1(b)(1)(i). Additionally, your Articles are silent regarding the disposition of your assets upon your dissolution, which also causes you to fail the organizational test per Treas. Reg. Section 1.501(c)(3)-1(b)(4).

You do not meet the operational test under IRC Section 501(c)(3) because you are not operating exclusively for exempt purposes as required under Treas. Reg. Section 1.501(c)(3)-1(c)(1). Your activities consist of organizing and operating an adult softball team, which is neither exclusively educational nor charitable.

You are unlike the organization described in Rev. Rul. 64-275 because you do not provide a training program which prepares participants for national and international competitions. You are also unlike the organizations described in Rev. Rul. 65-2 and Rev. Rul. 80-215 because your recreational activities are for adults only. However, you are similar to the organization described in Rev. Rul. 70-4, which did not qualify for exemption under IRC Section 501(c)(3), because you provide a recreational softball team for adults.

Your activities consist of organizing and operating an adult recreational softball team. Because you are operating for substantial non-exempt purposes, as described in Better Business Bureau of Washington, D.C., Inc., you are precluded from exemption under IRC Section 501(c)(3).

You are unlike the organization described in Hutchinson Baseball Enterprises, Inc. because you operate for substantial recreational and social purposes of your members. You are like the organizations described in Media Sports League, Inc. and Wayne Baseball Inc. because your social and recreational activities are substantial and preclude exemption under IRC Section 501(c)(3).

Conclusion
Based on the information provided, you do not qualify for exemption under IRC Section 501(c)(3) because you are neither organized nor operated exclusively for exempt purposes within the meaning of Section 501(c)(3). Your articles are silent regarding your purposes as well as how your assets will be distributed upon your dissolution, causing you to fail the organizational test. You fail the operational test because your recreational activities for adults further a substantial non-exempt purpose. Accordingly, you do not qualify for exemption under Section 501(c)(3).

If you agree
If you agree with our proposed adverse determination, you don't need to do anything. If we don't hear from you within 30 days, we'll issue a final adverse determination letter. That letter will provide information on your income tax filing requirements.

If you don't agree
You have a right to protest if you don't agree with our proposed adverse determination. To do so, send us a protest within 30 days of the date of this letter. You must include:

- Your name, address, employer identification number (EIN), and a daytime phone number
- A statement of the facts, law, and arguments supporting your position
- A statement indicating whether you are requesting an Appeals Office conference
- The signature of an officer, director, trustee, or other official who is authorized to sign for the organization or your authorized representative
- The following declaration:

For an officer, director, trustee, or other official who is authorized to sign for the organization: Under penalties of perjury, I declare that I have examined this request, or this modification to the request, including accompanying documents, and to the best of my knowledge and belief, the request or the modification contains all relevant facts relating to the request, and such facts are true, correct, and complete.

Department of the Treasury
Internal Revenue Service
Tax Exempt and Government Entities
PO Box 2508
Cincinnati, OH 45201

Number: 202105009
Release Date: 2/5/2021

Date:
November 10, 2020
Employer ID number:

Form you must file:

Tax years:

Person to contact:
Name:
ID number:
Telephone:

UIL: 501.00-00, 501.03-05, 501.03-30

Dear :

This letter is our final determination that you don't qualify for exemption from federal income tax under Internal Revenue Code (IRC) Section 501(a) as an organization described in IRC Section 501(c)(3). Recently, we sent you a proposed adverse determination in response to your application. The proposed adverse determination explained the facts, law, and basis for our conclusion, and it gave you 30 days to file a protest. Because we didn't receive a protest within the required 30 days, the proposed determination is now final.

Because you don't qualify as a tax-exempt organization under IRC Section 501(c)(3), donors generally can't deduct contributions to you under IRC Section 170.

We may notify the appropriate state officials of our determination, as required by IRC Section 6104(c), by sending them a copy of this final letter along with the proposed determination letter.

You must file the federal income tax forms for the tax years shown above within **30 days** from the date of this letter unless you request an extension of time to file. For further instructions, forms, and information, visit www.irs.gov.

We'll make this final adverse determination letter and the proposed adverse determination letter available for public inspection after deleting certain identifying information, as required by IRC Section 6110. Read the enclosed Notice 437, Notice of Intention to Disclose, and review the two attached letters that show our proposed deletions. If you disagree with our proposed deletions, follow the instructions in the Notice 437 on how to notify us. If you agree with our deletions, you don't need to take any further action.

If you have questions about this letter, you can call the contact person shown above. If you have questions about your federal income tax status and responsibilities, call our customer service

Letter 4038 (Rev. 5-2020)
Catalog Number 47632S

Appendix #2

Department of the Treasury
Internal Revenue Service
P.O. Box 2508
Cincinnati, OH 45201

Release Number: 201645017
Release Date: 11/4/2016
UIL code: 501.36-00

Date: August 11, 2016

Employer ID number:

Contact person/ID number:

Contact telephone number:

Form you must file:

Tax years:

Dear :

This letter is our final determination that you don't qualify for tax-exempt status under Section 501(c)(3) of the Internal Revenue Code (the Code). Recently, we sent you a proposed adverse determination in response to your application. The proposed adverse determination explained the facts, law, and basis for our conclusion, and it gave you 30 days to file a protest. Because we didn't receive a protest within the required 30 days, the proposed determination is now final.

Because you don't qualify as a tax-exempt organization under Section 501(c)(3) of the Code, donors can't deduct contributions to you under Section 170 of the Code. You must file federal income tax returns for the tax years listed at the top of this letter using the required form (also listed at the top of this letter) within 30 days of this letter unless you request an extension of time to file.

We'll make this final adverse determination letter and the proposed adverse determination letter available for public inspection (as required under Section 6110 of the Code) after deleting certain identifying information. Please read the enclosed Notice 437, *Notice of Intention to Disclose*, and review the two attached letters that show our proposed deletions. If you disagree with our proposed deletions, follow the instructions in the Notice 437 on how to notify us. If you agree with our deletions, you don't need to take any further action.

We'll also notify the appropriate state officials of our determination by sending them a copy of this final letter and the proposed determination letter (under Section 6104(c) of the Code). You should contact your state officials if you have questions about how this determination will affect your state responsibilities and requirements.

Letter 4038 (Rev. 7-2014)
Catalog Number 47632S

If you have questions about this letter, you can contact the person listed at the top of this letter. If you have questions about your federal income tax status and responsibilities, call our customer service number at 1-800-829-1040 (TTY 1-800-829-4933 for deaf or hard of hearing) or customer service for businesses at 1-800-829-4933.

Sincerely,

Jeffrey I. Cooper
Director, Exempt Organizations
Rulings and Agreements

Enclosures:
Notice 437
Redacted Letter 4036, *Proposed Adverse Determination Under IRC Section 501(c)(3)*
Redacted Letter 4038, *Final Adverse Determination Under IRC Section 501(c)(3) - No Protest*

Letter 4038 (Rev. 7-2014)
Catalog Number 47632S

Department of the Treasury
Internal Revenue Service
P.O. Box 2508
Cincinnati, OH 45201

Date: June 20, 2016

Employer ID number:

Contact person/ID number:

Contact telephone number:

Contact fax number:

UIL:
501.36-00

Legend:
B = Date
C = Date
D = State
F = Organization
G = Organization
H = City
J = Date
K = Program
L = Program
x dollars = Amount

Dear :

We considered your application for recognition of exemption from federal income tax under Section 501(a) of the Internal Revenue Code (the Code). Based on the information provided, we determined that you don't qualify for exemption under Section 501(c)(3) of the Code. This letter explains the basis for our conclusion. Please keep it for your records.

Issues
Do you qualify for exemption under Section 501(c)(3) of the Code? No, for the reasons described below.

Facts
You were formed as a nonprofit corporation on B in the State of D. Per your Amended and Restated Charter filed on C, you were formed for the following purposes which the Charter states shall be exclusively religious, charitable, or educational within the meaning of section 501(c)(3) of the Code:

(i) Proclaiming earnestly the gospel message and to urge its personal acceptance.
(ii) Promoting prayer, Bible study, missions, Christian fellowship, evangelism, Christian service and encouraging, in every possible way, a lifetime commitment to Christ.

Letter 4036 (Rev. 7-2014)
Catalog Number 47630W

(iii) Providing a forum in which the Gospel of Jesus Christ can be discussed with non-believers outside of a formal church setting.
(iv) Generously extending the grace of God by giving away 100% of all profits (except those retained for capital expenditures) to community ministries, other local, national or international non-profits or organizations, or those in financial need.

Your Bylaws and Executive Summary also list the same four purposes.

The Minister of F, who is one of your founding board members, came up with the vision to form a coffee shop where believers could interact with non-believers in a safe and friendly environment to convey the Gospel in a non-confrontational manner in word and deed. You were formed as a separate entity from F in order to encourage other Christian churches and organizations to participate in your vision. F granted the funding for your start up and your board members are all members of F. Article 3, Section 2, of your Bylaws indicates that at least one of your directors must be an Elder of F. Additionally, a majority of your directors should be members of F.

Once you legally formed, you proceeded with your plan and opened a coffee shop in J using the business name G. You own the trademark to your logo and tagline. You sell coffee locally and plan to eventually sell it online as well. You state in your Executive Summary that the coffee house will exist for four purposes in your community:

1. give away 100% of profits,
2. provide a safe, inviting, and informal gathering place,
3. serve excellent coffee, espresso drinks, light fare, and
4. help revitalize downtown H.

Your Executive Summary also states that you believe the location of the coffee house is ideal for the following reasons:

- There is no other similar business in downtown.
- There is an unmet need in the downtown area for a gathering space that is open late and offers the community a safe place to gather.
- The previous renter also sold coffee and the general setup is close to what we envision as a helpful footprint.

Your website states that your mission is,

You are committed to giving away 100% of your profits to community based non-profit organizations and individuals who are already doing great work. You decided to not create another nonprofit community organization that did what other existing organizations already do well but rather help them expand their services by providing them with financial support.

You are open Monday through Friday from 6 a.m. to 8 p.m. and Saturday from 7 a.m. to 8 p.m. You have free Wi-Fi and power outlets throughout for customer use. You use coffee that is sourced directly from coffee farmers. Therefore, the coffee you buy benefits the coffee farmers 50-100% over the price paid for "Fair Trade" coffee. Your drink selection includes coffee, tea, smoothies, frappes, soft drinks, and juices. Your food items include baked goods, soups, sandwiches, salads, and desserts. Copies of your menu can be found on your website. The menu shows the various food and beverages you serve and the prices you charge for each. You also plan to sell your roasted coffee beans online in the future but you do not have the capability at this time. Your customers can currently purchase roasted beans at the coffee shop.

You state that at the coffee shop you provide a location for both formal and informal Bible study, church group meetings, and meetings for other organizations. So far, your location has been used for a Women's Bible Study, a Men's Bible Ministry, meetings of the Elders of F, book signings, birthday parties, baby and bridal showers, community business meetings, game nights, live music, and similar events. You do not typically charge a fee for the use of space by groups or organizations but your General Manager advises users that a "suggested" donation in the amount of x dollars per hour is welcome. You have never denied access or use of your room due to an inability to pay or a decision not to donate.

You stated that your promotion of the Gospel of Jesus Christ is subtle and indirect. Several times a year the Gospel has been promoted through a program referred to as "L". This program consists of a donor paying for a certain amount of coffee in advance. Then, when a customer comes in they are told by the staff that the coffee has already been paid for and, "that the coffee is not "free" but that the price has already been paid for it – *just like Jesus already paid the price for all of our sins by dying on the cross for us.*"

You also have your "Monthly Mission" where you partner with other ministries, missionaries, and non-profit organizations by regularly highlighting their activities to help raise funds, supplies, and recognition for them. You select a "partner" and provide information about the person or organization to your customers on display in your shop, on social media, and at F. You also collect donations for your partner. This has occurred on a quarterly basis. You have also been able to give away some items to other organizations for their fundraising events. You have donated coffee and gift baskets. You also give away meals and drinks to the homeless and help connect them with local ministries for lodging and jobs.

You previously took part in a training program that helps train underserved youth by placing them in a local business for a six week internship so they can gain firsthand experience.

You have participated with F in the K program which is a prison ministry that connects you and your customers to children with incarcerated parents. The program allows your customers to share gifts with the children and the true message of Christmas at a party bringing together the children, their caregivers, your staff, and customer angels at F. You have also participated in multiple community activities.

You have a Fund-giving Policy that explains how you will select the recipients of your funds. First, you have an application that organizations must complete that asks for their IRS classification, description of activities, and what they will do with the funds received. Every six months your board will review the applications and select two applicants. The two applicants selected will each receive half of the fundraising and proceeds from operations for six months. You will distribute funds to the recipient organizations every three months. There is no maximum to the amount that you will distribute but it will be limited to the money received from fundraising and the proceeds from your operations that exceed operating expenses, debts, and capital expenditures.

Your activities are run by compensated staff as well as volunteers. You estimated that approximately 15% of the total time expended toward your operations has been provided by volunteers. Volunteers help with operational aspects to promote the Gospel of Jesus Christ through service, roasting beans for G, assisting in waiting on customers and interacting with them, and helping with the maintenance and physical needs of the shop and equipment. Your Board Members regularly participate with planning your activities and the members of F generously give to assist with your operations and utilize the coffee shop as a forum for Christian fellowship.

Almost all of your revenue is from the sale of food items. Your largest expense is for salaries and wages. You also have occupancy expenses and expenses for cost of goods sold, advertising, licenses and permits, insurance, supplies, payroll, and repairs and maintenance. You have not yet earned profits that have allowed you to give away any substantial amount of money but you hope to be able to do that in the near future. F continues to provide donations to you to assist with your operations.

Law

Section 501(c)(3) of the Internal Revenue Code provides, in part, for the exemption from federal income tax of organizations organized and operated exclusively for charitable, religious or educational purposes, no part of the net earnings of which inures to the benefit of any private shareholder or individual.

Treasury Regulation Section 1.501(c)(3)-1(a)(1) states that, in order to be exempt as an organization described in section 501(c)(3) of the Code, an organization must be both organized and operated exclusively for one or more of the purposes specified in such section. If an organization fails to meet either the organizational test or the operational test, it is not exempt.

Treas. Reg. Section 1.501(c)(3)-1(c)(1) provides that an organization will be regarded as "operated exclusively" for one or more exempt purposes only if it engages primarily in activities which accomplish one or more of such exempt purposes specified in section 501(c)(3) of the Code. An organization will not be so regarded if more than an insubstantial part of its activities is not in furtherance of an exempt purpose.

Treas. Reg. Section 1.501(c)(3)-1(d)(2) provides that the term "charitable" is used in section 501(c)(3) of the Code in its generally accepted legal sense and includes relief of the poor and distressed or of the underprivileged as well as the advancement of religion.

Rev. Rul. 68-72, 1968-1 C.B. 250, states that a nonprofit organization that operates a supervised facility to bring together young people of college age with church leaders, educators, and leading businessmen of the community may be exempt from federal income tax under Section 501(c)(3) of the Code. The organization was formed by local churches for the purpose of furthering the religious, intellectual, and moral development of persons of college age through the operation of the "coffee house", a supervised facility where church leaders, educators, and leading businessmen of the community meet and mingle with young people in an informal atmosphere. They hold discussions on such subjects as religion, current events, and social problems. Personal counseling and vocational guidance are provided. A nominal charge is paid upon admission, but there are no additional charges for the refreshments and entertainment. The organization meets it expenses from contributions and the admission charges.

Rev. Rul.71-581, 1971-2 C.B. 236, stated that an organization that operated a thrift store where substantially all of the merchandise sold had been contributed and where more than half of the work performed at the thrift shop was performed without compensation, may be exempt under Section 501(c)(3) of the Code. The organization was organized by a group of nonprofit organizations exempt under Section 501(c)(3). The primary purpose for which the organization was formed was to serve the group of exempt organizations by performing an essential function for them of soliciting contributions of goods on their behalf and converting the contributed goods to cash for charitable uses.

Department of the Treasury
Internal Revenue Service
P.O. Box 2508
Cincinnati, OH 45201

Release Number: 201645017
Release Date: 11/4/2016
UIL code: 501.36-00

Date: August 11, 2016

Employer ID number:

Contact person/ID number:

Contact telephone number:

Form you must file:

Tax years:

Dear :

This letter is our final determination that you don't qualify for tax-exempt status under Section 501(c)(3) of the Internal Revenue Code (the Code). Recently, we sent you a proposed adverse determination in response to your application. The proposed adverse determination explained the facts, law, and basis for our conclusion, and it gave you 30 days to file a protest. Because we didn't receive a protest within the required 30 days, the proposed determination is now final.

Because you don't qualify as a tax-exempt organization under Section 501(c)(3) of the Code, donors can't deduct contributions to you under Section 170 of the Code. You must file federal income tax returns for the tax years listed at the top of this letter using the required form (also listed at the top of this letter) within 30 days of this letter unless you request an extension of time to file.

We'll make this final adverse determination letter and the proposed adverse determination letter available for public inspection (as required under Section 6110 of the Code) after deleting certain identifying information. Please read the enclosed Notice 437, *Notice of Intention to Disclose*, and review the two attached letters that show our proposed deletions. If you disagree with our proposed deletions, follow the instructions in the Notice 437 on how to notify us. If you agree with our deletions, you don't need to take any further action.

We'll also notify the appropriate state officials of our determination by sending them a copy of this final letter and the proposed determination letter (under Section 6104(c) of the Code). You should contact your state officials if you have questions about how this determination will affect your state responsibilities and requirements.

Letter 4038 (Rev. 7-2014)
Catalog Number 47632S

and corporate nature. The organization paid significant advertising and promotional expenses and derived substantial income from weddings and special events held at its conference center. The court determined that the organization's activities competed with a number of commercial, as well as non-commercial entities, which strongly evidenced a commercial nature and purpose. The court concluded that although the organization carried out a number of charitable and educational activities, these were incidental to its primary activity of operating a for-profit conference center.

In Zagfly, Inc. v. C.I.R., T.C. Memo 2013-29, the court held that Zagfly's primary activity, the operation of a web-based broker that would sell flowers at market rates, was not a charitable activity, but rather a commercial activity that amounts to an unrelated trade or business. Therefore, the organization did not meet the requirements of Section 501(c)(3) of the Code because its primary activity did not further a 501(c)(3) purpose.

Application of law

You are not described in Section 501(c)(3) of the Code nor Treas. Reg. Section 1.501(c)(3)-1(a)(1) because you fail the operational test. Specifically, the facts show you are not operated exclusively for Section 501(c)(3) purposes because a substantial portion of your activities consists of the operation of a coffee shop in a commercial manner.

While donating funds to other non-profit community organizations is charitable as described in Treas. Reg. Section 1.501(c)(3)-1(d)(2), your main focus is the operation of a coffee shop. Additionally, while some of the activities that take place in the coffee shop such as the "L" aim to advance religion, more than an insubstantial portion of your activities serve a commercial purpose. Per Treas. Reg. Section 1.501(c)(3)-1(c)(1), you are not regarded as "operated exclusively" for one or more exempt purposes because you do not engage primarily in activities which accomplish one or more of such exempt purposes specified in section 501(c)(3) of the Code. Your primary activity is the operation of a coffee shop in a commercial manner. You are open to the public Monday through Friday from 6 a.m. to 8 p.m. and Saturday from 7 a.m. to 8 p.m. You have free WiFi and power outlets throughout for customer use. You have space that can be used for gatherings such as meetings and parties. You have a selection of food and beverage items that can be purchased at the coffee shop. Your hours and menu can be found on your website and your Executive Summary indicates that you believe the location of the coffee house is ideal because there are no other similar businesses downtown. Therefore, the operation of your coffee shop to raise funds is a commercial activity, not a charitable activity.

Additionally, you do not meet the requirements of Reg. 1.501(c)(3)–1(c)(1) because more than an insubstantial amount of your activities are furthering non-exempt purposes. Your operation of a coffee shop consists of providing food and beverage to the public for a fee. You are similar to the organization in Better Business Bureau of Washington, D. C., Inc. v. United States, in that you have a substantial commercial purpose to operate a coffee shop which is not in furtherance of any exempt purpose within the meaning of Section 501(c)(3). You are also similar to the organization in B.S.W. Group, Inc. v. Commissioner because your primary purpose is commercial. Your coffee shop resembles a trade or business that is ordinarily carried on by commercial ventures organized for profit. You chose your location because there is no other similar business downtown. You charge fees for your food and beverages and plan to eventually sell your coffee beans online.

You are distinguishable from the organization in Rev. Rul. 68-72 in that the majority of your activities are to operate your coffee shop in a commercial manner. The organization in Rev. Rul. 68-72 ran a supervised facility where church leaders, educators, and leading businessmen of the community met and mingled with young people in an informal atmosphere. They held discussions on such subjects as religion, current events, and social problems. Personal counseling and vocational guidance were provided. You do not conduct any regular religious or educational activities at your facility. While activities such as Bible studies may be conducted at your coffee shop, they are not conducted by you. They are conducted by groups that are coming to use your space. You allow your space to be used by the public for all activities, not just those that are religious, charitable, or educational. For instance, business meetings, birthday parties, and baby and bridal showers have all taken place at your coffee shop. Additionally, unlike the organization in Rev. Rul. 68-72 that charged a nominal admission fee but did not charge for refreshments or entertainment, you charge for the food and beverages at your shop. The majority of your expenses which are devoted to the operation of the coffee shop are met by the funds from these sales.

You are distinguishable from Revenue Ruling 71-581 in that the products sold at your coffee shop are not donated and only 15% of the work performed at the coffee shop is from volunteers. While you may have the common goal of donating the funds you make for charitable purposes, you stated that you have not yet earned profits that have allowed you to give away any substantial amount of money. Even if you do, contributing net profits to charity does not make a business exclusively charitable.

You are similar to the organization described in Rev. Rul. 73-127 because the operation of the coffee shop and your programs to further the Gospel of Jesus Christ, partner with other organizations, and participate in community activities are separate and distinct activities. Since the operation of the coffee shop is a substantial part of your activities and is not a recognized charitable purpose, you are not organized and operated exclusively for 501(c)(3) purposes.

You are not similar to the organization ruled in Rev. Rul. 76-94 because the operation of your coffee shop is your main function and your planned religious and charitable programs are secondary to your overall coffee shop activities.

You are similar to the organizations described in the American Institute for Economic Research v. United States, B.S.W. Group, Inc. v. Commissioner, Airlie Foundation v. I.R.S., Living Faith, Inc. v. Commissioner, and Zagfly, Inc. v. C.I.R. because you have a significant non-exempt commercial purpose. You are operating a coffee shop that is open to the public six days a week in competition with other commercial markets. This is indicative of a business. Your primary sources of revenues are from coffee shop sales. Your expenses are mainly for salaries, cost of goods sold, and occupancy expenses to support the operation of the coffee shop. Taking in totality, the operation of your coffee shop constitutes a significant non-exempt commercial activity.

Conclusion

Based on the facts and circumstances presented, we conclude that you do not qualify for recognition of exemption from federal income tax as an organization described in Section 501(c)(3) of the Code. Your coffee shop activities are indistinguishable from similar activities of an ordinary commercial enterprise.

If you don't agree

You have a right to file a protest if you don't agree with our proposed adverse determination. To do so, you must send a statement to us within 30 days of the date of this letter. The statement must include:

- Your name, address, employer identification number (EIN), and a daytime phone number
- A copy of this letter highlighting the findings you disagree with

- An explanation of why you disagree, including any supporting documents
- The law or authority, if any, you are relying on
- The signature of an officer, director, trustee, or other official who is authorized to sign for the organization, or your authorized representative
- One of the following declarations:

  For an officer, director, trustee, or other official who is authorized to sign for the organization:
  Under penalties of perjury, I declare that I examined this protest statement, including accompanying documents, and to the best of my knowledge and belief, the statement contains all relevant facts and such facts are true, correct, and complete.

  For authorized representatives:
  Under penalties of perjury, I declare that I prepared this protest statement, including accompanying documents, and to the best of my knowledge and belief, the statement contains all relevant facts and such facts are true, correct, and complete.

Your representative (attorney, certified public accountant, or other individual enrolled to practice before the IRS) must file a Form 2848, *Power of Attorney and Declaration of Representative*, with us if he or she hasn't already done so. You can find more information about representation in Publication 947, *Practice Before the IRS and Power of Attorney.*

We'll review your protest statement and decide if you provided a basis for us to reconsider our determination. If so, we'll continue to process your case considering the information you provided. If you haven't provided a basis for reconsideration, we'll forward your case to the Office of Appeals and notify you. You can find more information about the role of the Appeals Office in Publication 892, *How to Appeal an IRS Decision on Tax-Exempt Status*.

If you don't file a protest within 30 days, you can't seek a declaratory judgment in court at a later date because the law requires that you use the IRS administrative process first (Section 7428(b)(2) of the Code).

Where to send your protest
Please send your protest statement, Form 2848, if needed, and any supporting documents to the applicable address:

U.S. mail:

Internal Revenue Service
EO Determinations Quality Assurance
Room 7-008
P.O. Box 2508
Cincinnati, OH 45201

Street address for delivery service:

Internal Revenue Service
EO Determinations Quality Assurance
550 Main Street, Room 7-008
Cincinnati, OH 45202

You can also fax your statement and supporting documents to the fax number listed at the top of this letter. If you fax your statement, please contact the person listed at the top of this letter to confirm that he or she received it.

If you agree

If you agree with our proposed adverse determination, you don't need to do anything. If we don't hear from you within 30 days, we'll issue a final adverse determination letter. That letter will provide information on your income tax filing requirements.

You can find all forms and publications mentioned in this letter on our website at www.irs.gov/formspubs. If you have questions, you can contact the person listed at the top of this letter.

Sincerely,

Director, Exempt Organizations

Enclosure:
Publication 892

Letter 4036 (Rev. 7-2014)
Catalog Number 47630W

Appendix #3

Department of the Treasury
Internal Revenue Service
Tax Exempt and Government Entities
IRS

Number: **202242011**
Release Date: 10/21/2022

UIL: 501.03-00

Date: May 14, 2021

Taxpayer ID number:

Form:

Tax periods ended:

Person to contact:
Name:
ID number:
Telephone:
Fax:

CERTIFIED MAIL - RETURN RECEIPT REQUESTED Number:

Dear :

Why we are sending you this letter
This is a final determination that you don't qualify for exemption from federal income tax under Internal Revenue Code (IRC) Section 501(a) as an organization described in IRC Section 501(c)(3), effective . Your determination letter dated , is revoked.

Our adverse determination as to your exempt status was made for the following reasons:

Your organization was formed to promote the conditions of life throughout the world by engaging in fundraising and making donations to other IRC Section 501(c)(3) organizations that have similar objectives. Your organization fails to meet the organizational test because its nonprofit corporate status has been revoked by the state in which it was incorporated, . In addition, you have not conducted any fundraising activities, or received any public support for a period of five consecutive years. Organizations described in IRC Section 501(c)(3) of the Code and exempt under IRC Section 501(a) must be both organized and operated exclusively for exempt purposes. You have not demonstrated that you are organized and operated exclusively for charitable, educational, or other exempt purposes within the meaning of IRC Section 501(c)(3).

Organizations that are not exempt under IRC Section 501 generally are required to file federal income tax returns and pay tax, where applicable. For further instructions, forms and information please visit www.irs.gov.

Contributions to your organization are no longer deductible under IRC Section 170.

What you must do if you disagree with this determination
If you want to contest our final determination, you have 90 days from the date this determination letter was mailed to you to file a petition or complaint in one of the three federal courts listed below.

How to file your action for declaratory judgment
If you decide to contest this determination, you may file an action for declaratory judgment under the provisions of IRC Section 7428 in one of the following three venues: 1) United States Tax Court, 2) the United States Court of Federal Claims or 3) the United States District Court for the District of Columbia.

Letter 6337 (12-2020)
Catalog Number 74808E

Please contact the clerk of the appropriate court for rules and the appropriate forms for filing an action for declaratory judgment by referring to the enclosed Publication 892, How to Appeal an IRS Determination on Tax-Exempt Status. You may write to the courts at the following addresses:

United States Tax Court	U.S. Court of Federal Claims	U.S. District Court for the District of Columbia
400 Second Street, NW	717 Madison Place, NW	333 Constitution Ave., N.W.
Washington, DC 20217	Washington, DC 20439	Washington, DC 20001

Processing of income tax returns and assessments of any taxes due will not be delayed if you file a petition for declaratory judgment under IRC Section 7428.

Information about the IRS Taxpayer Advocate Service

The IRS office whose phone number appears at the top of the notice can best address and access your tax information and help get you answers. However, you may be eligible for free help from the Taxpayer Advocate Service (TAS) if you can't resolve your tax problem with the IRS, or you believe an IRS procedure just isn't working as it should. TAS is an independent organization within the IRS that helps taxpayers and protects taxpayer rights. Contact your local Taxpayer Advocate Office at:

Internal Revenue Service
Taxpayer Advocate Office

Or call TAS at 877-777-4778. For more information about TAS and your rights under the Taxpayer Bill of Rights, go to taxpayeradvocate.irs.gov. Do not send your federal court pleading to the TAS address listed above. Use the applicable federal court address provided earlier in the letter. Contacting TAS does not extend the time to file an action for declaratory judgment.

Where you can find more information

Enclosed are Publication 1, Your Rights as a Taxpayer, and Publication 594, The IRS Collection Process, for more comprehensive information.

Find tax forms or publications by visiting www.irs.gov/forms or calling 800-TAX-FORM (800-829-3676).

If you have questions, you can call the person shown at the top of this letter.

If you prefer to write, use the address shown at the top of this letter. Include your telephone number, the best time to call, and a copy of this letter.

Keep the original letter for your records.

Sincerely,

Sean E. O'Reilly
Director, Exempt Organizations Examinations

Enclosures:
Publication 1
Publication 594
Publication 892

cc:

Letter 6337 (12-2020)
Catalog Number 74808E

About the Author

Rev. John P. Joseph, Esq., CCA Emeritus is an ordained minister with the Assemblies of God, attorney, and Certified Church Business Administrator (CCA) and Fellow in Church Business Administration (Emeritus) now called The Church Network. He completed his undergraduate studies at Stetson University in 1982 and earned his Juris Doctorate degree from the University of Kentucky, College of Law in 1986. John also received a Cambridge Certificate in Risk Management for Churches and Schools from Cambridge University, England in 2000. He has been a member of the Florida Bar since 1986 and is admitted to practice in every state court in the State of Florida and the United States Tax Court. As the founder and principal attorney at the Church Legal Center in Minneola, Florida John represents many churches, ministries, and charities across the state of Florida.

"Unlock more content by John Joseph"

SCAN ME

www.ingramcontent.com/pod-product-compliance
Lightning Source LLC
LaVergne TN
LVHW071338210926
848486LV00003B/171